SPECIAL FORCES
LAND VEHICLES

SPECIAL FORCES
LAND VEHICLES

MRAPS • MOTORCYCLES • ALL-TERRAIN VEHICLES

ALEXANDER STILWELL

amber
BOOKS

Published by Amber Books Ltd
United House
London N7 9DP
United Kingdom
www.amberbooks.co.uk
Facebook: amberbooks
Instagram: amberbooksltd
Twitter: @amberbooks
Pinterest: amberbooksltd

ISBN: 978-1-83886-166-7

Editor: Michael Spilling
Designer: Mark Batley
Picture research: Terry Forshaw

Printed in Thailand

CONTENTS

INTRODUCTION

The vehicles used by special forces have provided them with the speed and mobility to carry out their unique style of warfare. The iconic World War II Jeep enabled the first special forces, the Special Air Service (SAS), to make lightning raids on enemy installations and airfields. Later, Land Rover and similar 4x4 vehicles would enable special forces worldwide to carry out similar roles. However, no conflict is exactly the same and special forces, as well as their vehicles, have adapted to different kinds of warfare and terrain.

This book is divided into six different categories of special forces vehicles based upon their primary focus and purpose. There is some overlap but overall the selection reflects the fact that, even in the same conflict region, special forces may have to engage in different types of environments, the most obvious being an open rural or desert environment versus a densely populated urban one.

The focus of the book is vehicles in current or recent use, bearing in mind that a vehicle type that has been stood down by one military establishment may be taken up by another. Chapter 1 begins with legacy vehicles that in so many ways still provide a point of reference for how special forces vehicles have evolved over more recent years. The attempts to up-armour some of these vehicles were in response to the new threat of asymmetric warfare represented by the improvised explosive device (IED) and the mine in the conflicts that took place in Afghanistan and Iraq. The need to provide better protection for special forces and conventional troops led to the urgent development and fielding of Mine Resistant Ambush Protected (MRAP) vehicles, which are covered in Chapter 2. Some designs, such as the HMT 400, attempted to strike a balance between protection and visibility, which in itself is a form of protection. The problem of armour weight versus mobility was sometimes tackled by providing appliqué armour kits that could be fitted according to mission requirements.

In Chapter 3, which covers light all-terrain vehicles, we move back into more familiar territory. Despite the increased threats from mines and IEDs, there is still a place in the special forces inventory for light, fast vehicles that are easily air transportable and deployable. In this case, the vehicles and their occupants are protected by their ability to approach their targets via unpredictable routes and over difficult terrain with reduced danger of coming across mines or IEDs. The range and mobility of these low-signature vehicles also enables the delivery aircraft to stand off from the mission area and reduce the danger of identification by enemy radar.

One of the reasons for the success of the Long Range Desert Group that operated in North Africa during World War II was its ability to stay on station for long periods. This was due to the fact that the group included supply trucks with spare water, food, ammunition and other essentials. Resupply by primary units can compromise a long-range reconnaissance mission, although these may need to be carried out on occasion for longer missions. Chapter 4 describes some of the vehicles that are used for this important supply role, including those that can be extended to carry a larger payload and go the extra mile.

LONG RANGE DESERT GROUP
Chevrolet 30cwt trucks were widely used by the LRDG on desert operations. Note the Browning machine gun and the extended rod wireless aerial for communications far from base.

HMMWV
US Navy SEALs lay down
covering fire with an M240
machine gun during a
capabilites exercise.

Although 'technicals', or commercial vehicles, armed with a range of weapons, including a heavy machine gun, have been a feature of war among poorly resourced insurgents and other groups for a long period of time, the War on Terror, particularly in Afghanistan and Iraq, threw a spotlight on the use of commercial vehicles by special forces. In the early months of the conflict in Afghanistan, commercial vehicles, including the locally available Toyota Hilux or Land Cruiser 4x4s, were converted on the spot by special forces, including improvised mounts for M2 .50 calibre machine guns or similar weapons.

As time went on, United States Special Operations Command (USSOCOM) formalized the use of such vehicles by buying Toyota Tacomas, the US version of the Hilux, in the United States and upgrading them at Fort Campbell. This included beefed up suspensions, body armour and fittings for advanced communications. Similar conversions continue to be carried out by a variety of contractors for US and other special forces. A similar vehicle was also developed, the Purpose-Built Special Operations Tactical Vehicle (PB-SOTV), a military vehicle designed to mimic commercial vehicles. The Non-Standard Commercial or Tactical Vehicle says so much about the adaptability of special forces and their need to keep a low profile. It may be worth noting in this context that overtly militarized commercial vehicles, such as the Toyota Land Cruiser-based Jankel Fox Rapid Reaction Vehicle (RRV) in service with Belgian special operations forces, are described in Chapter 4 under support vehicles.

The military motorcycle has come a long way since it played a major role in the world wars of the twentieth century. Leaner and meaner, the military motorcycle is now used in a more focused way and is particularly well-suited to some special forces' roles, ranging from rapid airfield assessments by US Air Force Special Operations Command (AFSOC) special tactics personnel to forward reconnaissance. As you will see in Chapter 6, there have been some notable developments in motorcycle design tailor-made for special forces. If you did not think it was possible to reinvent the two-wheel motorbike, read that chapter and discover that this is exactly what they have done.

The motorbike's four-wheel cousin, the quad, has also found a role in special operations, ranging from support and supply to direct intervention. Some smaller manufacturers are competing with the established firms to provide bespoke quads for special forces.

BUSHMASTER
Soldiers take cover behind a Bushmaster Protected Mobility Vehicle as a CH-47 Chinook lifts off at Shoalwater Bay Training Area in North Queensland during Exercise Hamel 2018.

What special forces do

It may be useful to summarize the context in which special forces use the vehicles described in this book. Special forces are often involved in strategic reconnaissance, which involves gathering intelligence about enemy positions and deployments, as well as information about their assets and the ground that they occupy. Special forces are well suited to this role due to their specialist training and ability to infiltrate covertly and extract themselves without being seen.

Special forces are also proficient at carrying out targeted asymmetric raids. Part of special forces DNA, the asymmetric raid means that the effect of a relatively small group of highly-trained operators can have a disproportionate effect. Not only can a highly-trained group cause significant damage, it can also tie down significant enemy resources as they try to counter similar raids in the future. To carry out such raids, special forces require vehicles that can take them to the objective with minimal chance of being identified, that have significant firepower to carry out the mission and that have the ability to extract them so that they do not have to get involved in an extended firefight with a larger enemy force.

This ability to operate with proficiency and speed also involves high levels of training with the equipment that is being used. This means thorough familiarity with the vehicles involved and training in how to use

FLYER 60

The Flyer 60 has most of the attributes of the Flyer 72 but in a narrower frame that allowed it to be carried internally in the CH-47 Chinook helicopter.

them to best effect. This includes knowing how to operate a vehicle in desert conditions, including deep sand, fording rivers, and how to use a two-wheel-drive or all-wheel-drive trail bike or an ATV or quad.

Special forces have often worked closely with local friendly groups. By winning hearts and minds they can maximize the effect of their relatively small presence on the ground. In this respect, using vehicles such as non-standard commercial vehicles can help special forces to blend into the local environment.

In urban counterterrorism or anti-insurgency operations, special forces may require vehicles that provide full protection from attacks from buildings and so on and which provide a platform for high-tempo operations against selected targets.

Whatever the mission, special forces will always select the vehicle best suited to the task and will demand the same levels of performance, endurance and adaptability that they demand of themselves.

DESERT PATROL VEHICLE
US Navy SEALs training with the Desert Patrol Vehicle. The DPV provided the speed and mobility that special forces often demand of their vehicles.

Intense training – both in SOF schools and units – is required to integrate competent individuals into fully capable units. This process cannot be hastened without degrading ultimate capability. – US Special Operations Command

LEGACY LIGHT UTILITY VEHICLES

The world's first special forces light vehicle was the iconic Jeep, or, to use its formal name, the US Army Truck ¼ ton 4x4 Command Reconnaissance. The preferred transport of the world's first special forces unit, the Special Air Service (SAS), in North Africa during World War II, the Jeep came to symbolize the spirit of elite fighting units worldwide. Fitted with twin Vickers machine guns, the SAS Jeeps made lightning raids on enemy airfields and other installations, causing devastation before disappearing as fast as they had arrived. Although the SAS was similar in some ways to the Long Range Desert Group (LRDG), operating in the same theatre at the same time, the Jeep represented the difference between the two units. Small and fast, the Jeep was quite different from the large Chevrolet and Ford trucks used by the LRDG on its missions.

LAND ROVER 110 SAS LIGHT VEHICLE

The Land Rover 110 and 90 were a mainstay for British forces for many years but proved to be vulnerable to the effects of IEDs and mines.

After the end of the North Africa campaign, the SAS continued to use Jeeps effectively in Italy, and after the D-Day landings in northern Europe, where British, French and Belgian SAS units made life as difficult as possible for the German defenders.

SAS use

By 1948, no doubt inspired by the Jeep, the Rover Company developed its own 4x4 light utility vehicle, the Series I Land Rover. Unlike the Jeep, which had been produced according to a US military specification, the Land Rover was a civilian vehicle primarily aimed at farmers and other users requiring a tough outdoors vehicle. It also had a roof and doors. However, it did not take long for the British Ministry of Defence (MoD) to recognize the potential for this new vehicle. Although the MoD had been developing its own light utility vehicle in the form of the Austin Champ, there were development problems. The Land Rover seemed to have everything the MoD wanted. Initial military orders soon quadrupled and the relationship between the company and the British armed forces was firmly established – and continues to this day.

WILLYS JEEP
The Jeep was the most successful 4x4 vehicle of World War II. Its speed and mobility made it a popular vehicle with early special forces units.

The SAS recognized that the Land Rover had the same DNA as their original Jeeps, while also providing more space for equipment and weapons. Before long, the Land Rover-made Long Range Desert Patrol Vehicle, otherwise known as the Pink Panther due to its desert camouflage pink paintwork, was carrying SAS units.

In 1952, the SAS became part of the regular army, following a spell as a Territorial Army regiment, and was initially equipped with the Austin Champ as a replacement for the Jeep. The Champ was fitted with a Vickers machine gun and a .303 Bren gun, and trailers were attached to carry extra equipment. When the rest of the army moved over to the Land Rover, so did the SAS. In 1955 it acquired the Series I Land Rover, which it used until 1967, when it was given the Series IIA Land Rover. This had a 2.25-litre petrol engine and a 109mm (4.3in) wheelbase. It was fitted with twin Bren guns on the front and a .50 calibre Browning heavy machine gun on the rear. Mortar tubes were fitted beneath the radiator grille. A spotlight was fitted next to the driver. Both doors and the windscreen were removed and there were racks for carrying jerry cans. For desert use, the Land Rovers were painted a shade of pink. This was an idea inherited from the Long Range Desert Group in World War II, who had discovered that pink was the best camouflage colour in desert conditions. As a result, their vehicles were known as Pink Panthers, or 'Pinkies', a name somewhat at odds with their power and performance.

CHEVROLET TRUCK
A Chevrolet 30cwt of the Long Range Desert Group armed with a Lewis gun at the rear and a .303 Browning Mk II at the front. the truck carries sand channels on the side of the rear compartment.

Land Rover 110 DPV

In 1985, the SAS acquired the new Land Rover 110 High Capacity Pick-Up (HCPU) as its Desert Patrol Vehicle (DPV). The Land Rover HCPU was fitted with coil-spring suspension and powered by a 3.5-litre V8 diesel engine. It was capable of carrying more powerful weaponry than its predecessor, including a 7.62mm (0.3in) General Purpose Machine Gun (GPMG), a .50 calibre Browning heavy machine gun, a Mk 19 40mm (1.6in) grenade launcher and a MILAN wire-guided missile launcher. Smoke canisters were fitted both front and rear. The 110 was later renamed the Defender, in line with Land Rover rebranding.

'PINK PANTHER' LAND ROVER
A Land Rover 110 modified for use by the UK SAS. Note the 7.62mm (0.3in) GPMGs at the front and rear of the vehicle. Sand channels are carried on the sides and it is fitted with a snorkel exhaust for deep water.

LAND ROVER 110 'PINKIE'
The Land Rover 'Pinkie' was used by the SAS during the first Gulf War. It had the capacity to carry enough personal equipment for long range patrols in the desert.

During the Gulf War of January–February 1991, the SAS, along with its US special forces counterparts, played a crucial role in tracking down and destroying the tactical ballistic missiles known as Scuds, which had been targeted mainly at Israel and whose use threatened to destroy the fragile Arab coalition against Iraq by provoking Israeli retaliation. A and D Squadrons of the SAS deployed into Iraq using Land Rover 110 'Pinkie' Desert Patrol Vehicles, accompanied by trail bikes for forward reconnaissance. Using night sights to maintain anonymity and concealing the vehicles in gullies with camouflage, the SAS contributed to a successful mission against Scud deployments, either by destroying the missiles and their launchers directly or by bringing in air support.

The Land Rover 110 vehicles were not available to all the SAS patrols. Given the option of using the smaller Land Rover 90, or Dinky, SAS patrol Bravo Two Zero opted to deploy on foot. The decision appears to have contributed to the disaster that befell the patrol when it was compromised by the enemy. Of the eight men in the patrol, four were captured, one was killed in action, two died of hypothermia and one escaped. The weight of equipment packed into Bergen rucksacks, including observation equipment, weapons and ammunition, proved to be a major problem for the patrol and when it came to exfiltration, a lack of vehicles meant this had to be attempted on foot in freezing conditions.

Other military forces around the world were quick to also recognize the potential of the Land Rover. Some adapted the basic Land Rover chassis for their own purposes and others developed their own vehicles. US Special Operations Command developed its Ground Mobility Vehicle (GMV) from the High Mobility Multipurpose Wheeled Vehicle (HMMWV), or Humvee, while the Mercedes Benz G-Wagen, created with Steyr-Puch, became the basis of the Interim Fast Attack Vehicle (IFAV) manufactured for the US Marine Corps, and of the Peugeot P4 used by French special forces.

Both the Land Rover and the G-Wagen were, to some extent, wolves in sheep's clothing, at least in their standard versions. The extensive modifications ordered by the British MoD for the Land Rover Defender, such as strengthened suspension, were not obvious on the surface and this Wolf version formed the basis of the Weapons Mount Installation Kit (WYMIK), the revised RWYMIK and the Snatch/Vixen Land Rover.

Whereas the Jeeps and Land Rover Pink Panthers had been ideal for roving the wide-open deserts, operations in Iraq and Afghanistan presented a new challenge – the Improvised Explosive Device, or IED. Although attempts were made to improve armour protection, the days of the traditional Military Light Utility Vehicle seemed to be numbered by the early 1990s. The tension between the need for speed and agility, which was so much a part of the special forces' creed, and the requirement for armoured protection in the face of new types of asymmetric warfare, would henceforth be a challenge for military minds.

Snatch/Vixen Land Rover

Snatch/Vixen Land Rovers were based on an armoured GVW Ricardo Land Rover CD 110 chassis. This included an armoured belly plate between the front seats, as well as improved suspension.

Snatch Land Rovers were first used by British Army security 'snatch' squads in Northern Ireland. When deployed in Iraq and Afghanistan,

LAND ROVER 110
Country of origin:
United Kingdom
Manufacturer: Land Rover
Service: 1983–2000
Operators: British Army
Crew: 4
Weight: 1600kg (3527lb)
Dimensions: Length: 4m (15ft)
Width: 1.79m (5ft 11in) Height
2.1m (7ft)
Powerplant: 3.5 litre Rover V8
Range: 573km (356 miles)
Speed: 160km/h (99mph)
Weapons: N/A

SNATCH/VIXEN LAND ROVER

Country of origin: United
Kingdom

Manufacturer: Land Rover

Service: 1992–present

Operators: British Army

Crew: 4

Weight: 4050kg (8930lb)

Dimensions: Length 4.55m (14ft
11in), Width 1.79m (5ft 10in),
Height 2.03m (6ft 8in)

Powerplant: Land Rover 4 300
turbo diesel injection

Range: 510km (317 miles)

Speed: 97km/h (60mph)

Weapons: N/A

however, despite their armour protection and electronic countermeasures, they proved vulnerable to roadside bombs. They were eventually replaced by specialist mine-protected vehicles (MPVs).

The Snatch Land Rover became the catalyst in the growing controversy as to whether armoured vehicles could provide adequate protection for military personnel. The argument would run and run in both the UK and the US, whose military forces bore the brunt of mines and IEDs in both Iraq and Afghanistan. As a result of continuing pressure from families of servicemen, the UK placed orders for vehicles similar to the US Cougar, namely the Mastiff and Ridgeback. However, the direct replacement for the Snatch Land Rover under the UK Light Protected Vehicle (LPV) programme would be the Ocelot/Foxhound, manufactured by Force Protection Europe (see Chapter 2).

Land Rover Weapons Mount Installation Kit (WMIK)
The Land Rover WMIK is based on the 110 Truck Utility Medium, otherwise known as the Land Rover Wolf. The WMIK version was developed

by Land Rover and Ricardo Vehicle Engineering. It incorporates roll cages and weapon mounts. The vehicle is designed to carry a variety of optional weapons, including medium and heavy machine guns, grenade launchers and a MILAN anti-tank missile launcher. Later versions were developed to carry the Automatic Lightweight Grenade Launcher (ALGL).

Deployment of the vehicle in Iraq and Afghanistan revealed the WMIK's vulnerability to IEDs. In 2011, the Revised Weapons Mount Installation Kit (RWMIK) was introduced. This featured a Modular Armour Protection Kit (MAPK) as passive defence, and electronic countermeasures (ECM) as active defence.

Land Rover WMIKs have been used by various elite British units during conflicts, including the invasion of Iraq under Operation Telic in 2003. The WMIKs were used by the Pathfinder Platoon, a reconnaissance element of 16 Air Assault Brigade, in both Iraq and Afghanistan. The vehicles were also used by the Royal Marines Brigade Reconnaissance Force (Brigade Patrol Group). When the British 3 Commando Brigade was deployed in Gamsir, Southern Helmand, in Afghanistan in 2007, during an operation against a major Taliban stronghold, the Brigade Patrol Group mounted in Land Rover WMIKs was tasked with conducting reconnaissance. It drove close enough to the enemy to draw fire in what is called armoured reconnaissance and was able to establish the strength of the enemy position.

Range Rover

The British Special Air Service (SAS) used specially adapted Range Rovers as command and control vehicles, or as transport to incidents. Modified Range Rovers carried a support platform for building entry. Other

---

LAND ROVER WMIK

Country of origin: United Kingdom

Manufacturer: Land Rover Special Vehicles Operation

Service: 2000–present

Operators: British Army

Crew: 4

Weight: 4100kg (9039lb)

Dimensions: Length 4.55m (14ft 11in) Width 1.79m (5ft 10in) Height 2.03m (6ft 7in)

Powerplant: Land Rover 4 300 turbo-diesel injection

Range: 510km (317 miles)

Speed: 160km/h (99mph)

Weapons: Rear: .50 calibre heavy machine gun; 40mm GMG grenade launcher; 7.62mm (0.3in) GPMG; MILAN anti-tank missile launcher; front: pintle-mounted 7.62mm (0.3in) GPMG

modifications included run-flat tyres, armour plating and infrared headlights. Many of the modifications to Range Rovers were invisible, which would have allowed SAS teams to move around inconspicuously. The agility and speed of the Range Rover, whether on or off road, made it an ideal choice for rapid and adaptable movement.

The SAS discontinued its use of Range Rovers for more practical tasks in the mid-1990s when the Range Rover range became ever more tailored to the luxury user.

Land Rover Perentie Long Range Patrol Vehicle (LRPV)

The Land Rover Perentie was an adapted version of the Land Rover Defender built in response to an Australian Army tender to replace the Series II and Series III Land Rovers. Produced from 1987, the Perentie vehicles came in both 4x4 and 6x6 versions. They were fitted with Isuzu 3.9-litre four-cylinder diesel engines. The chassis was galvanized and the spare tyre was moved beneath the rear load area.

The Australian Special Air Service Regiment (SASR) version was based on the Perentie 6x6 and included a central ring mount that could be fitted with an M2 .50 calibre Browning heavy machine gun or a Mk 19 automatic grenade launcher. There was a mount for a MAG 58 medium machine gun near the front passenger seat. The vehicle could also carry a Suzuki DRZ 250cc trail motorbike for scouting. Designed for patrolling the huge Australian Outback, the Perentie LRPV proved highly effective on

1982 RANGE ROVER
The SAS used early versions of the Range Rover for low-profile reconnaissance and observation duties as well as a command-and-control vehicle. During operations in Afghanistan and elsewhere, however, they used more practical 4x4s.

deployment in both Iraq and Afghanistan. In 1991, the SASR was deployed in LRPVs to Kuwait in Operation Desert Thunder. They were later deployed to Afghanistan in Operation Slipper (2002) and to Iraq in Operation Falconer (2003). In 2002 a LRPV hit a land mine, destroying the vehicle. One soldier was killed and the other two personnel in the vehicle were injured. As a result, LRPVs were fitted with a Survival Enhancement Kit, which included armour plating underneath the vehicle and shock absorption in the seats.

In 2003, the Australian SASR deployed in LRPVs across the Iraqi border from Jordan as part of a joint special forces patrol that included the UK SAS and the US 1st Special Forces Operational Detachment-Delta (SFOD-D).

Land Rover Perentie 4x4 Surveillance Reconnaissance Vehicle

This variant of the LRPV was operated by the Australian 2nd Commando Regiment, which worked in support of the SASR. The Surveillance Reconnaissance Vehicle (SRV) was also fitted with a central ring mount in the back that could mount an M2 Browning .50 calibre machine gun or a Mk 19 automatic grenade launcher. There was in addition a mount at the front for a MAG 58 machine gun.

By 2008, the LRPV was largely replaced by the Bushmaster and the Australian Army had placed an order for the Supacat HMT Extenda, which would become fully operational in 2012.

The SASR carried out vehicle-mounted patrols in Land Rover Perenties during Operation Slipper, the Australian contribution in the war against al-Qaeda and the Taliban in Afghanistan. Their main role was vehicle-mounted reconnaissance, which made best use of the Perentie's long range and mobility over challenging terrain. As part of Task Force 58, they operated with US Marines in Kandahar and Helmand.

Under Operation Falconer, the Australian SASR used Perenties as part of Combined Joint Special Operations Task Force West (CJSOTF). One troop

LAND ROVER PERENTIE
The 6x6 configuration of the Land Rover Perentie enabled it to carry a large payload for long-range missions. It is fitted with a Mk 19 grenade launcher on the central weapons mount and a .50 calibre Browning machine gun at the front of the vehicle.

LONG-RANGE PATROL
Land Rover Perentie long-range patrol vehicles on patrol in Afghanistan. The primary weapons are pointed in alternate directions to provide maximum security for the patrol column.

LAND ROVER PERENTIE LONG RANGE PATROL VEHICLE (LRPV)
Country of origin: Australia
Manufacturer: JRA Ltd
Service: 1989–present
Operators: Australian Special Air Service Regiment (SASR)
Crew: 3
Weight: 3660kg (8069lb)
Dimensions: Length 6.10m (20ft), Width 2.2m (7ft 2in), Height 2.76m (9ft ½in)
Powerplant: Isuzu 3.9-litre 4-cylinder diesel engine
Range: 1600km (1000 miles)
Speed: 95km/h (59mph)
Weapons: M2 Browning machine gun, or Mk 19 grenade launcher, or Heckler & Koch general machine gun; MAG 58 MG

drove across the border while another was inserted with its vehicles by US Army MH-47E helicopters, demonstrating the transportability of the Land Rover Perentie. Later, they mounted an attack on the Al-Assad air base where they captured or destroyed enemy jet fighters.

Ground Mobility Vehicle (GMV), based on the HMMWV

Following its experience during the war in Iraq in 1991 and Operation Desert Storm, the US special operations community developed its own tailored versions of the standard M1025 and M1113 High Mobility Multipurpose Wheeled Vehicle (HMMWV), or Humvee. Designed to replace the venerable Jeep, first manufactured by Willys in World War II and redesigned by Ford as the Mi51, the Humvee came into service in 1986 and remains in use in various forms in both the US armed forces and other armed forces around the world.

The Humvee is about 60cm (2ft) wider than the Land Rover Defender and has a low centre of gravity, along with independent suspension. This makes it a very effective off-road vehicle but impractical in tight, built-up areas or narrow roads. The lack of armour protection on the base Humvee design meant that, like other soft-skin military vehicles, it was not suited for

HMMWV HYBRID
US Navy SEALs training with the HMMWV-based GMV-N vehicle. Note that the doors have been removed, makng the vehicle more easily accessible to operators.

urban combat or asymmetric warfare. This became apparent when Humvees
were involved in Mogadishu under Operation Restore Hope in 1992–93,
when US Rangers came under fire from multiple angles from small arms
and rocket-propelled grenades (RPGs). When armour kits were fitted
to Humvees it placed a strain on the chassis, among other problems.
Armoured turrets increased the danger of the vehicle rolling over.

In due course, the US military ordered interim mine-resistant vehicles
to replace the Humvee in certain combat conditions, while the longer-
term replacement was the Joint Light Tactical Vehicle (JLTV). However,
the Humvee continues to be used in various guises and is likely to remain
in service through to 2050.

Desert Mobility Vehicle (DMV)

The Desert Mobility Vehicle (DMV) was the Humvee component of
special operations in desert environments which would typically be
operated by US special forces and by 1st Special Forces Operational
Detachment-Delta (SFOD-D) in particular.

GMV Special Forces variants

The various special operations and elite units of the US Army, Navy and
Air Force developed their own versions of the Humvee Ground Mobility
Vehicle. They all had various characteristics in common, including
strengthened chassis and suspension, more rugged tyres with central tyre
inflation and improved off-road capability. Other features included extra
fuel tanks, ammunition, food and water racks, an internal fire-suppression
system, smoke-grenade launchers, satellite communications, infrared (IR)
headlights and a radiator adapted for desert operations. The back of the
GMV was open so that mission-specific equipment and stores could be
carried.

The special forces Humvees were designated:
- GMV-S for US Army Special Forces
- GMV-R for the 75th Ranger Regiment
- GMV-N for US Navy SEALs
- GMV-T/GMV-SD/GMV-ST for US Air Force Special Operations
  Command
- GMV-M for US Marines Special Operations Command

Other Special Operations Forces (SOF) that used the GMV included
the Canadian Joint Task Force 2 (JTF-2) and the New Zealand SAS
(NZSAS).

GMVs can carry a range of armaments, including an M2 .50 calibre
machine gun, an M240 machine gun, a Mk 249 machine gun, and a
Mk 10 or Mk 47 40mm (1.6in) grenade launcher, as well as smoke-
grenade launchers. The GMVs feature a swing-arm weapon mount on

GROUND MOBILITY VEHICLE-N (GMV-N)
Country of origin: United States
Manufacturer: AM General
Service: 1991–present
Operators: US Navy SEALs; US Marine Corps Special Operations Command (MARSOC); Air Force Special Operations Command (AFSOC); 75th Ranger Regiment
Crew: 4
Weight: Not known
Dimensions: Length 4.57m (15ft), Width 2.16m (7ft 1in), Height 1.53m (6ft)
Powerplant: VG 6.5 litre turbocharged diesel engine
Range: 443km (275 miles)
Speed: 110km/h (70mph)
Weapons: M2 .50 calibre Browning machine gun, or M240 machine gun or Mk 19 40mm (1.6in) grenade launcher, or M249 machine gun and smoke grenade launchers

NAVY SEALS GMV-N
US Navy SEALs manoeuvre with a Ground Mobility Vehicle (GMV-N). Note the swing-arm mount on the left-hand side of the vehicle which is fitted with an M240 machine-gun.

the passenger-side door frame for an M240 or M249. There is a second swing-arm at the rear that can support an M240 or M249, or an SOF Mk 48 machine gun.

The GMV can be fitted with modular armour if necessary, depending on mission specifics. For missions requiring greater speed and agility, armour can be left off. Although they preferred the unarmoured GMV, which was both light and agile, as the IED threat continued to develop SOF forces increasingly used up-armoured versions of the GMV. The Ground Mobility Vehicle-R was used by B Company 3rd Ranger Battalion, 75th Ranger Regiment, during the storming of the Al-Qadisiya (Haditha) dam complex north-west of Baghdad on 1 April 2003.

The objective was to secure the dam before the Iraqi regime under Saddam Hussein could breach it and slow down the US and Allied advance. The Rangers were operating in cooperation with special forces, in particular the 160th Special Operations Aviation Regiment (Night Stalkers). The Ranger convoy consisted of 17 GMV-R vehicles and 140 Rangers. The cross-country mobility of the vehicles was tested as they approached the dam and the ground became hilly and intersected by dry wadis. Time was pressing as they needed to reach their objective before daylight. Eventually, they reached a metalled road and the GMV-Rs grouped closer together as they sped along at 97km/h (60mph).

When the troops reached the objective and engaged with the enemy, one GMV-R took a wrong turn and ran into a group of Iraqi soldiers, who opened fire. The Ranger driver managed to reverse at high speed, despite having four flat tyres, and the Rangers on board escaped unscathed. The Rangers also used the .50 calibre machine guns and Mk 19 grenade launchers on the vehicles to neutralize enemy fire.

Ranger Special Operations Vehicle (RSOV)

The Ranger Special Operations Vehicle was developed after the US Rangers took an interest in the Land Rover Defenders used by British forces in the Gulf War. Seeking a replacement for the venerable M151 utility truck, a descendant of the World War II Jeep, and wanting something more nimble than the HMMWV 'Humvee', the Rangers ordered a customized Land Rover Defender 110. The RSOV features a weapons mount across the rear capable of hosting a range of arms, including the M60, M240 and M2 machine guns, or a Mk 19 grenade launcher. There is also a mount at the front for a weapon operated by the front passenger.

The RSOV can seat up to six armed Rangers. The vehicle can be carried by Chinook or EH-101 helicopters and by C-130 Hercules cargo planes. It can also be carried in slings under a helicopter.

Other versions include a communications vehicle, known as a 'Shark', a mortar carrier (MORTSON), or a medical vehicle (MEDSOV).

RANGER SPECIAL OPERATIONS VEHICLE (RSOV)
Country of origin: United Kingdom
Manufacturer: Land Rover
Service: 1992–present
Operators: 75th Ranger Regiment; Portuguese Army Commandos; Czech Republic; North Cyprus
Crew: 3–7
Weight: 7734lb (3508kg)
Dimensions: Length 4.41m (14ft 5in), Width 1.79m (5ft 9in), Height 1.93m (6ft 3in)
Powerplant: 4-cylinder turbo-charged diesel engine
Range: 500km (300 miles)
Speed: 160km/h (99mph)
Weapons: M2 .50 calibre Browning machine gun; M240 7.62mm (0.3in) machine gun; Mk 19 40mm grenade launcher

Pinzgauer High-Mobility All-Terrain Vehicle (4x4 and 6x6)

The Pinzgauer ATV is a successful all-terrain vehicle originally produced by Steyr-Daimler-Puch in Austria. Later versions, including the Pinzgauer II, were produced by BAE Systems in the UK. With its all-wheel drive and high clearance, with options for either 4x4 or 6x6 versions, the Pinzgauer was highly adaptable as a transporter for troops and supplies. The Pinzgauer 718 6x6 was selected by the New Zealand Defence Force (NZDF) in 2005 to replace its fleet of Land Rovers and the order included versions for the New Zealand Special Air Service (NZSAS). Special Forces Operational Detachment-Delta (SFOD-Delta), or Delta Force, employed Pinzgauer 6x6 vehicles to provide mobility during operations in Afghanistan. The Delta Force Pinzgauers can be

PINZGAUER ATV
British soldiers train with a FGM-148 Javelin anti-tank guided missile fired from the back of a Pinzgauer at the Salisbury Plain Training Area.

mounted with a range of weapon systems, including M2 machine guns, M240 and M299 belt-fed machine guns, and Mk 19 grenade launchers.

Vector Light Protected Patrol Vehicle (LPV)

The Vector was an armoured version of the Pinzgauer 718 6x6 which was designed to provide improved protection for UK forces deployed to Afghanistan following the shortcomings of the Land Rover Snatch vehicles when faced with IEDs. It featured Kevlar armour protection and it also provided more cover and greater carrying capacity.

Deployed from 2007, the Vector did not, however, provide sufficient protection against the IED threat in Afghanistan and the vehicles were soon withdrawn.

PINZGAUER HIGH-MOBILITY ALL-TERRAIN VEHICLE

Country of origin: Austria/United Kingdom

Manufacturer: Steyr-Daimler-Puch/BAE Systems

Service: 1971–present

Operators: British Army; New Zealand Defence Force and New Zealand SAS; US Special Operations Command Delta Force

Crew: 6

Weight: Not known

Dimensions: Length 5.3m (17ft 4in), Height 2m (6ft 6in), Width 1.8m (5ft 9in)

Powerplant: Steyr 4-cylinder petrol engine or 6-cylinder diesel

Range: 400km (248 miles)

Speed: 4x4 110km/h (62mph); 6x6 160km/h (99mph)

Weapons: M2 Browning .50 calibre heavy machine gun; 2 x 7.62mm (0.3in) M60 machine guns

PINZGAUER ATV
The Pinzgauer ATV proved to be a robust, reliable support vehicle that was also used by US and New Zealand Special forces for reconnaissance.

IFAV
The Interim Fast Attack Vehicle proved to be a robust and easily accessible solution for the US Marine Corps. Based on a proven Mercedes chassis, it could be internally transported in a US Marine Corps CH-53 Sea Stallion helicopter.

Interim Fast Attack Vehicle (IFAV)

The Interim Fast Attack Vehicle (IFAV) was commissioned by the US Marine Corps to equip its Marine Expeditionary Units (Special Operations Capable), or MEU (SOC), including Marine Force Recon.

The IFAV was brought in to replace the ageing M151-A2 Jeep Fast Attack Vehicle (FAV), which had demonstrated several deficiencies in its role. US Marine deployments worldwide demanded an urgent replacement before a longer-term solution could be found, and in May 1999 a rapid fielding requirement was issued. The acquisition programme soon identified the proven Mercedes MB290GT long-bed

Operation Enduring Freedom

Many of the vehicles mentioned in this book were deployed during the global War on Terror that followed the attack by al-Qaeda on the United States on 11 September 2001, which resulted in about 3,000 deaths.

President George W. Bush stated at the time that any nation harbouring terrorists would be considered an enemy. As al-Qaeda was operating at that time from Afghanistan, the Taliban regime in that country was identified as an adversary. On 7 October 2001, Operation Enduring Freedom was launched with the objective of destroying al-Qaeda in Afghanistan and defeating the Taliban regime. NATO nations were involved in support of the United States under Article 5 of the NATO treaty, which states that any attack on a NATO member is regarded as an attack on all states. Special forces and intelligence units from the US and UK started to operate in Afghanistan from September 2001 and the US 5th Special Forces Group was inserted in October 2001 in northern Afghanistan as part of Task Force Dagger.

Special forces from NATO and other coalition nations included US Special Operations Command, UK special forces, the Australian SASR, the New Zealand SAS, Canada's Joint Task Force 2, Norway's Haerens Jegerkommando, Denmark's Jeger Corps, the German KSK, and elite forces such as the US Marines Force Recon, the US 75th Ranger Regiment, the British Royal Marines, the British Army Parachute Regiment, the Netherlands Marine Corps, and the French 1er, 3e, 21 Régiment d'Infanterie de Marine.

AUSTRALIAN SAS
Soldiers of the Australian SASR in a Land Rover Perentie Long Range Patrol Vehicle after capturing Al-Asad air base as part of Operation Falconer.

INTERIM FAST ATTACK VEHICLE (IFAV)

Country of origin: Austria/
Germany
Manufacturer: Magna Steyr/
Mercedes-Benz
Service: 2000–present
Operators: US Marine Corps
Crew: 3
Weight: 1990kg (4387lb)
Dimensions: Length 4.8m (15ft
8in), Height 2.1m (6ft 8in), Width
1.84m (6ft ½in)
Powerplant: 2.9 litre turbo-
charged diesel
Range: not known
Speed: 96km/h (58mph)
Weapons: M249 Squad
Automatic Weapon; M2 .50
calibre Browning machine gun;
Mk 19 40mm (1.6in) grenade
launcher; TOW missile system

'Gelundeswagon' as the most suitable basis for an 'off-the-shelf' vehicle to be moulded to specific Marine requirements. Armored Vehicle Systems Inc. and Daimler Chrysler adapted the vehicle to make it capable of water-fording and also provided roll-over safety. Specific 360-degree weapon mounts were also fitted and the vehicle was equipped with floor armour to provide ballistic protection against grenades and anti-personnel mines.

The IFAV could mount a range of weapons, such as the M249 Squad Automatic Weapon, the M2 .50 calibre Browning machine gun, the Mk 19 40mm (1.6in) grenade launcher and the TOW (Tube-launched, Optically tracked, Wire-guided) missile system. The IFAV could be carried by CH-46 Sea Knight and CH-53 Sea Stallion helicopters, and the V-22 Osprey tiltrotor aircraft.

The IFAV remained in service until 2009, when it was replaced by the M161 Growler Internally Transportable Light Strike Vehicle (ITV-LSV).

The Interim Fast Attack Vehicle (IFAV) was involved in an early US Marines Corps intervention in Afghanistan on 25–26 November 2001, when the 15th Marine Expeditionary Unit (Special Operations Capable), or MEU (SOC), flew from USS Peleliu and USS Bataan. The IFAVs were operated by 17 Force Recon, whose task was to secure the objective, namely Forward Operating Base (FOB) Rhino, about 137km (85 miles) southwest of Kandahar. With their vehicles and 66 Marines loaded on six CH53E Sea Stallion helicopters, the force departed the ships at sunset and, due to the length of the journey, had to refuel on the way. After arriving at the destination amid a brownout (the dust thrown up by the helicopters' blades), the Force Recon units dashed out with their IFAVs to secure the area. They had just completed the longest amphibious raid in history.

Peugeot P4/Panhard Véhicule Patrouille SAS (VPS)

The Peugeot P4 was commissioned by the French Army to replace its Jeeps dating back to the 1960s. Based on the chassis of the Mercedes G-Wagen, the basic P4 was fitted with a Peugeot 504 engine and gearbox.

The Commandement des forces spéciales Terre (French Special Forces Command), ordered an upgraded vehicle that could withstand long-range operations, mainly in desert conditions. This would be used by special operations units such as the 1er Régiment de Parachutistes d'Infanterie de Marine (RPIMa) and the 13e Régiment de Dragons Parachutistes. RPIMa became part of the SAS during World War II as a Free French force based in the UK and it remains proud of that association.

The P4 has significant Mercedes-Benz components, including the engine and gearbox, and it has been modified to include armour plating on the underside, a roll-over bar and a 360-degree mount in the back capable of taking a 12.7mm (0.5in) machine gun, as well as smaller calibres. The VPS can also mount a MILAN anti-tank missile unit and there is a 7.62mm (0.3in) machine gun mount at the front. The VPS is small enough to be carried in aircraft such as the C-160 Transall or the C-130 Hercules.

The VPS can carry up to five soldiers, including the driver, with all their combat gear, while also having sufficient room to carry supplies, water and ammunition.

PEUGEOT P4/PANHARD VÉHICULE PATROUILLE SAS (VPS):

Country of origin: France
Manufacturer: Panhard/ Mercedes-Benz
Service: 1982–present
Operators: French special forces
Crew: 5
Weight: 4000kg (8818lb)
Dimensions: Length 4.87m (15ft 10in), Width 2.21m (7ft 2in), Height 2.5m (8ft 2in)
Range: 800km (497 miles)
Speed: 95km/h (59mph)
Weapons: 12.7mm (0.5in) machine gun; 7.62mm (0.3in) machine gun

PROTECTED VEHICLES

Protected vehicles are a particular feature of conflicts with insurgents. Some of the most effective early versions of protected vehicles were developed in the 1970s by Rhodesian and South African military forces. Vehicles such as the Casspir included the now familiar V-shaped hull, along with enhanced armour.

During the wars in Iraq and Afghanistan, casualties suffered by coalition forces as a result of IEDs led to urgent requests for specifically designed armour-protected vehicles, especially when the limitations of upgraded versions of standard 4x4 light vehicles such as the HMMWV and the Land Rover became apparent.

ARQUUS SABRE
A soldier fires a Missile Moyenne Portée (MMP) from an Arquus Sabre vehicle. Relatively light special forces vehicles such as the Sabre are able to deploy considerable firepower.

In 2007, the United States began its Mine Resistant Ambush Protected (MRAP) programme in order to field protected vehicles. The programme included smaller and lighter vehicles designed for urban operations as well as those designed for special forces. In June 2007, for example, BAE Systems received orders for more than 300 variants of the RG-33 MRAP vehicle for use by US Special Operations Command (USSOCOM).

MRAP vehicles

Although MRAP (or equivalent) British protected vehicles provided greater protection against IEDs than up-armoured versions of the US HMMWV or British Land Rover, they also had several disadvantages. The most obvious was their sheer weight and bulk, along with top-heavy dynamics, making them vulnerable to tipping over in canals or collapsing bridges. The personnel inside were often facing inwards and were therefore unable to see what was going on around them. Nor were they able to defend themselves through firing ports. The vehicles were often cramped inside and personnel were liable to be thrown around when travelling over rough terrain.

CASSPIR

The Casspir was an early example of a mine-resistant ambush-protected vehicle. Note the high ground clearance and V-shaped hull, designed to minimize the effects of mine blasts.

As the draw-down of US forces in Iraq and Afghanistan continued, it became clear that the MRAP fleet of vehicles was largely surplus to requirements and efforts were made to sell them off to foreign military forces. The UK went through a similar process after its departure from Afghanistan in 2014, decommissioning the Mastiff, Ridgeback and Wolfhound vehicles as well as the remnant of the Land Rover Snatch/Vixen and RWYMIK fleets. The Foxhound and the new Boxer vehicles were maintained as replacements. For US forces, the M-ATV and the Joint Light Tactical Vehicle (JLTV) were designed to be the way forward for armour-protected vehicles that also provided sufficient agility, manoeuvrability and mobility. But the fact remained that these new vehicles were still very heavy and cumbersome compared with vehicles such as the HMMWV and Land Rover that they were designed to replace.

MASTIFF
Based on the US Cougar vehicle, the Mastiff is a heavily armed patrol vehicle that was used by British forces on operations in Afghanistan.

Bushmaster Infantry Mobility Vehicle (IMV)/Protected Mobility Vehicle (PMV)

After a somewhat complex development period, the Bushmaster Infantry Mobility Vehicle (IMV) came into service with the Australian Defence Force in 1997. The purpose of the vehicle is to provide protected transport for up to nine soldiers, along with a driver, to the operational area.

The vehicle has a V-shaped hull to protect against IEDs, can be fitted with an armour protection package to guard against shrapnel and small-arms fire up to 7.62mm (0.3in), has an armoured windscreen, and can also be fitted with electronic countermeasures to provide active security.

Additional features include air conditioning, a cool drinking-water system, personal weapons storage and a communications station. It has lockable roof hatches, which can be used as firing ports or as emergency escape hatches.

There are gun mounts on the single front and two rear hatches that can be fitted with a 7.62mm (0.3in) general purpose machine-gun, a 40mm (1.6in) grenade launcher or a .50 calibre Browning machine gun. The vehicle also has run-flat tyres and a central tyre inflation system. A protected extra fuel tank can be used in emergencies.

During operations in Afghanistan and elsewhere, the Bushmaster had a 100 per cent survivability rate, despite suffering numerous IED or mine incidents which sometimes wrote off the vehicles. However, the Bushmaster was not so heavily armoured that it lost its mobility. The Bushmaster could still be used on unpredictable off-road routes that lessened the danger of hitting explosive devices.

Other users of the Bushmaster include the Dutch Army and Royal Netherlands Marines, as well as the New Zealand Defence Force and the Indonesian and Japanese military.

Bushmaster MR6

A revised version of the Bushmaster, known as the MR6, includes reconfigurable troop seating, allowing greater mission adaptability; new doors on the front sides for the driver and commander; a wider rear door for faster access and exit; a new, more flexible, storage system; an anti-lock braking system (ABS); improved heavy-duty suspension; and a new digital dashboard for easier operation. It is also fitted with C4I (command and control, communications, computers and intelligence) systems, as well as an integral computing system (ICS), enabling the crew to manage weapons and sensors on the vehicle.

UK Special Forces (UKSF) Escapade

The UK Ministry of Defence ordered a limited number of Bushmasters for use by UK Special Forces (UKSF). The UKSF variant was known as the

MRAP FLEET

Soldiers from the US 10th Mountain Division maintain MRAP vehicles at the maintenance distribution yard on Kandahar Airfield, Afghanistan.

BUSHMASTER INFANTRY MOBILITY VEHICLE (IMV)
Country of origin: Australia
Manufacturer: Thales Australia
Service: 1997–present
Operators: Australian Defence Force; Royal Dutch Marines; UK Special Forces; Indonesian armed forces; Japanese armed forces
Crew: Driver, plus 9
Weight: 11,400kg (25,133lb)
Dimensions: Length 7.18m (23ft 5in), Width 2.48m (8ft 1in), Height 2.65m (8ft 7in)
Range: 800km (497 miles)
Speed: 100km/h (62mph)
Weapons: Remote Weapon Station (RWS) mounting 12.7mm (0.5in) HMG or 40mm (1.6in) automatic grenade launcher (AGL); front- and rear-manned swing mounts for 7.62mm (0.3in) machine guns

Escapade. The Escapade was adapted for use by the SAS in urban areas in order to provide full protection from IEDs and other threats. It featured additional armour protection, a remote weapons system (RWS), bull bars and an electronic countermeasures suite.

Operations

Bushmasters are thought to have been deployed in so-called Task Force Black operations in Iraq and Syria. These were rapid special forces missions designed to hunt down and interrogate suspected terrorist leaders. The Escapade vehicles enabled the SAS to improve interoperability with equivalent US special forces who were also deployed in fully protected vehicles. Bushmasters were also operated by the Australian Special Forces Task Group deployed to Afghanistan from 2005.

HMT 400 or Jackal

The HMT 400, known in the British Army as the Jackal, was designed to fulfil an urgent need to replace the conventional Land Rover WMIK and Snatch vehicles, which were challenged by long distances, difficult terrain and IEDs. This is why the HMT 400 was made with better cross-country ability, a greater carrying capacity and much improved armour protection. The special forces version was known as the Menacity.

HMT 400

A British Army Jackal is put through its paces in the desert at Camp Bastion, Afghanistan.

The new vehicle was fitted with a powerful Cummins 5.9 litre turbo-charged diesel engine and featured a revolutionary air suspension system

that afforded not only a comfortable ride across rough ground but also the ability to lower the vehicle to provide a stable platform for firing weaponry. Speed and agility allow the HMT 400 to carry out rapid reconnaissance or screening while also enabling it to move quickly away from danger. However, the HMT 400 is also fitted with an armour package that includes blast-attenuating seating.

The HMT 400's large storage capacity provides for extended patrols by special forces. The vehicle can be fitted with a range of weapons, including a .50 calibre heavy machine gun, Mk 19 or GMG 40mm (1.6in) grenade launchers or Javelin anti-tank missiles. The HMT 400 is compact enough to be carried inside a CH-47 Chinook helicopter, Atlas C.1 A400M or C-130 Hercules transport aircraft. It includes infrared headlight filters to be used with night vision goggles and run-flat tyres.

JACKAL 2
Soldiers from the 5th Battalion 'The Argylls' try out the new Jackal 2 armoured vehicle at the Long Valley Test Ground in Aldershot, Hampshire.

Jackal 2

The Jackal 2 featured a strengthened chassis and more powerful engine, which in turn meant that the vehicle could support a more elaborate composite armour protection package, especially on the sides, to provide protection from small-arms fire. The weapons mount was moved forwards to provide better arcs of fire, and there was space for a fourth crew member. Further improvements were incorporated in the Jackal 2A, including improved armour protection.

HMT 400/JACKAL

Country of origin:
United Kingdom

Manufacturer: Supacat

Service: 2008–present

Operators: British Army/
Royal Air Force

Crew: 4, plus 1

Weight: 6650kg (14,660lb)

Dimensions: Length 5.39m
(17ft 8in), Width 2m (6ft 7in),
Height 1.97m (6ft 6in)

Powerplant: 5.9 litre Cummins
ISBe Euro3

Range: Not known

Speed: 130km/h (81mph)

Weapons: M2 .50 calibre
Browning machine gun or
Heckler & Koch 40mm (1.6in)
GMG

Task Force Black

Task Force Black was a designation used for an SAS and Special Boat Service (SBS) component of the Joint Special Operations Command and Task Force in Iraq after the coalition invasion in 2003. The name was later changed to Task Force Knight.

Other special forces units operating under the same command included Task Force Blue, including US Navy SEALs and SEAL Team 6; Task Force Green, including 1st Special Forces Operational Detachment (Delta); and Task Force Orange, including US signals intelligence units.

Task Force Black and its partners ran coordinated operations that relied on good intelligence and speed of interception to strike at high-value insurgent leaders responsible for the bombing campaigns in Iraq. With the potential for being exposed to IEDs, small-arms fire and other forms of ambush, the SAS and other units relied on vehicles that could provide sufficient protection to go into and get out of dangerous areas.

Coyote

A larger version of the HMT 400, the six-wheel HMT 600, or Coyote, is essentially the same design but with more space. It can be used to support the lighter vehicles and replaced previous supply vehicles, such as the Unimog.

COYOTE
Instructors from the Specialist Training Division instruct members of the British 1st Queens Dragoon Guards to operate the Coyote protected vehicle during an eight day course.

Long Range Reconnaissance, 1940–2020

The development of long-range special forces vehicles such as the Supacat Extenda has its roots in the vehicles used by the Long Range Desert Group in World War II. Founded by Major Ralph Bagnold in June 1940, the Long Range Desert Group (LRDG) was conceived to carry out long-range reconnaissance and assaults against enemy targets during the North Africa Campaign fought by the British and German Afrika Korps. Manned by tough volunteers from New Zealand, Britain and India, the LRDG was first organized into six patrols and later into two squadrons.

One of the favourite vehicles of the LRDG was the Chevrolet 30cwt WB truck. This truck was specially adapted for its role and for desert conditions. It was fitted with a radiator condenser so as to preserve water in the hot environment and was stripped of all unnecessary weight, such as the doors and windscreen, in order to allow for extra stores and for the addition of weapons such as the Lewis gun, .303 Browning machine gun, Bofors gun or the Vickers anti-aircraft gun. The Chevrolet WB could travel 386km (240 miles) on a single tank and it was fitted with compasses, including a special sun compass, to help the crew with directions.

Although it did not have run-flat tyres such as those fitted to modern special forces vehicles, the crews learned to lower the tyre pressures when going through soft sand in order to maximize traction. Like its modern successors, the Chevrolet's suspension was strengthened so that it could carry the extra weight for long missions. Other vehicles used by the LRDG included the CMP light Ford 01 15cwt truck, the CMP Ford F30 cwt F30 4x4 truck, the Chevrolet 1533 x2 30 cwt truck, and the Willys Jeeps.

LRDG CHEVROLET
The World War II vintage Chevrolet truck has a similar layout and purpose to the special forces long range patrol vehicles of the 21st century.

Vehicles compared:	Chevrolet WB 30cwt	Supacat HMT Extenda
Max speed	80km/h (50mph)	120km/h (75 mph)
Range	386 km (240 miles)	1000km (621 miles)
Engine	216 CI 5-cylinder inline engine	Cummins 6.7 litre, 6-cylinder diesel
Dimensions (L/W/H)	5.3m (17ft 4in); 2.1m (6ft 9in); 1.8m (5ft 9in)	5.8m (19ft); 2.5m (8ft 3in); 0.85m (2ft 10in)
Weapons	Lewis gun; .303 Browning machine gun; Bofors gun; Vickers anti-aircraft machine gun	12.7mm (0.5in) heavy machine gun; 7.62mm (0.3in) machine gun; 40mm automatic grenade launcher

Operations

With its extended range, ample space, significant firepower and agility over rough terrain, the Jackal was an ideal vehicle for elite long-range reconnaissance and support for units such as the Parachute Regiment, Pathfinder Platoon and Royal Marines Brigade Patrol Troop, as well as reconnaissance units such as the Light Dragoons. Unlike some armoured vehicles, the Jackal transitioned successfully to other environments after the UK's draw-down from Afghanistan.

Special Forces Surveillance and Reconnaissance Vehicle/Offensive Action Vehicle (SRV/OAV), Menacity

UK Special Forces (UKSF), including the SAS Mobility Troop, deployed their version of the HMT 400, code-named the Menacity, from 2003. Special forces benefitted from the same characteristics as the elite regiments, including the extended range that enabled them to stay out longer on covert missions. It is thought that the vehicle has also been used by the 1st Special Forces Operational Detachment Delta (Delta Force).

Supacat Extenda

Based on the successful HMT 400 design, which was used by British special forces under the name Menacity, and by regular British forces as the Jackal, the Supacat Extenda was specifically designed as a special forces vehicle. The name derives from a unique feature whereby the vehicle can be extended from a 4x4 chassis to a 6x6 chassis (and converted back to a 4x4) in a relatively short time. It also includes a range of options regarding mission-

SUPACAT EXTENDA
Country of origin: United Kingdom
Manufacturer: SC Group
Service: 2017–present
Operators: Australian SASR; Norwegian special forces
Crew: 4
Weight: 9000kg/1200kg (19842lb/2646lb)
Dimensions: Length 5.8m/1.05m (19ft/3ft 4in), Width 2.05m (6ft 7in), Height 1.88m/2.44m (6ft 2in/8ft)
Powerplant: Cummins 6.7L, 6-cylinder diesel
Range: 1000km (621 miles)
Speed: 120km/h (75mph)
Weapons: 12.7mm (0.5in) machine gun; 7.62mm (0.3in) machine gun; 40mm (1/6in) automatic grenade launcher

specific hampers, weapons, ISTAR, communications and force protection equipment to suit a range of operational roles. Other features include run-flat tyres, a remote weapons station, smoke-grenade launchers and infrared lights.

The Supacat Extenda is now used by British special forces, as well as Australian and New Zealand special forces. These versions are manufactured in Australia by Supacat. It has also been deployed by the Norwegian Forsvarets Spesialkommando and Danish Spesialkorpset special forces, and is being considered by both the Czech Republic and Estonia.

The Supacat Mk 2 features an enhanced suspension system that allows the vehicle to carry a heavier payload, six crew rather than four, and also to incorporate a more effective blast and protection package.

RG-33 Mine Resistant Ambush Protected Vehicle

Based on the RG-31 vehicle developed by BAE Systems South Africa, the RG-33 was selected by the US Department of Defense to protect its forces in Afghanistan and Iraq against the threat of mines, IEDs and small-arms fire. BAE Systems developed a prototype for assessment by the Department of Defense in only seven months.

The vehicle design included versions for the US Army, US Marine Corps and US Special Operations Command (USSOCOM). In June 2008, BAE Systems was awarded a contract for 40 SOCOM RG-31 vehicles and this

RG-33 MINE RESISTANT
ARMOUR PROTECTED VEHICLE
Country of origin: South Africa
Manufacturer: BAE Systems
Service: 2008–present
Operators: US Special Operations Command; US Marine Corps
Crew: 8
Weight: 17,237kg (38,000lb)
Dimensions: Length: 6.7m (22ft 1in), Width 2.4m (8ft), Height 3.4m (11ft 3in)
Powerplant: Cummins 400 16 diesel
Range: Not known
Speed: 109km/h (68mph)
Weapons: M2 .50 calibre machine gun; Mk 19 40mm (1.6in) grenade launcher

was supplemented by an order for another 32 vehicles in August 2010. After deployment in Iraq and Afghanistan, the experiences learned from IED and mine incidents, including explosively formed penetrators, led to an upgrade in the passive appliqué armour package and tougher ballistic glass. The suspension was also upgraded for deployment in Iraq and Afghanistan.

Standard protection features on the RG-33 include a V-shaped hull, armour protection and TRAPP armoured glass in the crew compartment which allows visibility for the crew without compromising security. The special operations vehicle features an XM153 CROWS II (Common Remotely Operated Weapon Station). The turret is controlled remotely from within the vehicle and can be fitted with an M2 .50 calibre machine gun or a Mk 19 40mm (1.6in) grenade launcher. The CROWS system includes cameras and sensors that provide information in real time for the internal crew member remotely operating the weapon and enables them to put down accurate fire against any threats with the aid of a fire-control computer. The vehicle also includes C4I systems. Other features of the RG-33 include an automated fire-suppression system, a hydraulic ramp, a gunner's protection

M-ATV

US soldiers assigned to 91st Brigade Engineer Battalion begin movement in an Oshkosh M-ATV during training at the Hohenfels Training Area in Germany, February 2021.

kit, a robotic arm, mine-protected seating, air conditioning, dedicated space for equipment storage and run-flat tyres. The vehicle is powered by a Cummins 400 16 diesel engine and has an Allison 3200 transmission.

BAE Systems also delivered the RG-33 to the US Marines Corps after a contract was placed in February 2008. This complemented the other vehicles supplied to the US Marines by BAE Systems, namely the Caiman and RG-31.

MRAP All-Terrain Vehicle (M-ATV)

In 2008, the US Department of Defense began investigating a lighter form of Mine Resistant Ambush Protected Vehicle for deployment in Afghanistan. By June 2009, a single contract for the M-ATV had been awarded to Oshkosh, the manufacturer judged to have the vehicle with the best survivability, as well as the best production infrastructure. The vehicle included features such as a V-shaped hull, an engine fire-suppression system, central tyre inflation (CTIS), run-flat inserts, a traction-control system and anti-lock brakes. An optional remote weapon system could be fitted, including a top-mounted turret with a weapon that can be fired from within the vehicle. Weaponry may include an M2 .50 calibre machine gun, an M249 machine gun, a 40mm (1.6in) grenade launcher or an BGM 71 TOW missile launcher. The weapons are linked to a long-range target acquisition system. The vehicle is fitted with enhanced situational awareness (ESA) technology. A vision enhancer provides wide fields of view while minimizing blind spots. It optimizes navigation through difficult visual conditions such as fog, darkness or blown sand or dust. The system integrates with ultra-light thermal cameras, a vision enhancer and an ultra-wide vision system.

The M-ATV is fitted with energy-absorbing armour to the floor, seats and wheel arches, and also includes blast deflectors. The armour is designed to protect against Explosively Formed Penetrator (EFP) devices.

The TAK-4 independent suspension system provides excellent traction and mobility over rough terrain, with 40cm (16in) independent wheel travel and 33cm (13in) ground clearance. This provides better mobility than would be found in a vehicle with a straight axle. The M-ATV has a cruising range of approximately 500km (310 miles). The drive train is designed to cope with challenging conditions, including mud, sand, snow and deep water, and can operate at extreme temperatures, ranging from -32°C (-26°F) to 54°C (130°).

Several variants of the M-ATV were produced, including the M1245 and M1245A1 for special operations. These vehicles were designed with an emphasis on unconventional warfare and counter-insurgency operations, special reconnaissance and target acquisition. The SF variants included a protected cargo area, advanced C4ISR systems that provide the crew with optimum situational awareness and the ability to select the best operational options. These include IED-defeating systems as well as jammers.

MRAP ALL-TERRAIN VEHICLE (M-ATV)
Country of origin: United States
Manufacturer: Oshkosh
Service: 2009–present
Operators: US Special Operations Command (USSOCOM)
Crew: 4, plus driver
Weight: 12,500kg (27,500lb)
Dimensions: Length 6.27m (20ft 6in), Width 2.49m (8ft 2in), Height 2.7m (8ft 9in)
Powerplant: 7.2 litre 6-cylinder Caterpillar turbodiesel
Range: 500km (310 miles)
Speed: 105km/h (65mph)
Weapons: M2 .50 calibre Browning machine gun; M240 7.62mm (0.3in) machine gun; MK19 40mm (1.6in) grenade launcher; BGM 71 TOW anti-tank missile; MILAN anti-tank guided missile

M-ATV
An M-ATV of the 332nd Air
Expeditionary Wing is used
for security at an air base
somewhere in southwest Asia.

Ocelot/Foxhound Light Protected Patrol Vehicle (LPPV)

Due to the shortcomings of traditional Land Rovers, such as the Snatch, in the face of mines and IEDs, the British Army ordered a protected vehicle under its Light Protected Patrol Vehicle Programme that could have similar mobility to the Land Rover while offering significantly improved armour protection, as was offered by its larger vehicles, such as the Mastiff.

Designed by Force Protection Europe and the Formula 1 engineers' Ricardo, and manufactured by General Dynamics, the Foxhound was ordered by the British Army in 2010 under an urgent operational requirement. The first vehicles for testing were sent to Afghanistan in June 2012 after a remarkable design-to-delivery period of only two years.

Powered by a six-cylinder Steyr diesel turbocharged engine, the Foxhound has independent drive on all four wheels. It is claimed that the engine unit can be removed and replaced in under 30 minutes. The driving position provides good visibility and the six-speed automatic gearbox makes driving easy, enhanced by the four-wheel steering system.

FOXHOUND LPPV

A soldier from the Royal Irish Regiment fires his GPMG (General Purpose Machine Gun) from a Foxhound vehicle.

The V-shaped hull is designed to direct ground blasts away from the vehicle and it is fitted with composite armour to protect the crew from ballistic threats and explosive devices. The vehicle can carry four fully-equipped soldiers in addition to the driver and front passenger. The vehicle is compact enough to be moved in a C-130 transport aircraft or it can be underslung from a CH-47 Chinook helicopter.

There are two doors on each side at the front and one rear door. There are two hatches on the roof. Seating is provided for four personnel at the back, separated by a bulkhead from the driver and commander at the front. The vehicle is fitted with infrared technology and thermal imaging for inconspicuous movement in the dark. Internal screens provide 360-degree images of the area around the vehicle for situational awareness. There are mounts for two 7.62mm (0.3in) machine guns.

The Foxhound can be used for reconnaissance and special forces missions requiring fast insertion and extraction. Mission pods can be rapidly interchanged according to mission requirements.

Operations

The Foxhound was employed for force protection duties by the elite British Army Parachute Regiment in Afghanistan. Although apparently popular with the troops, there was some concern about the engine overheating in the intense heat.

Joint Light Tactical Vehicle (JLTV)

Designed to replace the High Mobility Multipurpose Wheeled Vehicle (HMMWV), the Joint Light Tactical vehicle (JLTV) was one of the results of the Mine Resistant Ambush Protected (MRAP) programme, which in turn was a response to the particular threats experienced by US military forces on deployment in Iraq and Afghanistan.

The first studies for the JLTV began in 2006 and, by 2015, having considered designs by several contractors, the Department of Defense awarded a contract to Oshkosh, whose design was considered to afford the best survivability and reliability at the most competitive cost. By June 2019, full-rate production had been approved by the US Army, which designated the JLTV as the platform for its Light Reconnaissance Vehicle (LRV) programme. The JLTV was also selected by the US Air Force for its Special Tactics forces. The US Marines acquired the JLTV for its expeditionary force to use worldwide. The JLTV was under consideration by the British Ministry of Defence for its Multi-Role Vehicle-Protected (MRV-P) programme for both the British Army and Royal Marines under foreign military sales. Discussions with the manufacturer included the potential for inserting UK-manufactured components, such as radios, in the vehicle.

Despite the initial enthusiasm of the US Army and US Marines for the new vehicle, both forces decided to keep the HMMWV in service alongside the new vehicle. As the US force draw-down from the Middle East continued, it became clear that a lighter vehicle such as the HMMWV was still appropriate for use in areas such as the European theatre, where the threat of mines and IEDs was not so significant. This appeared to raise the question as to whether the JLTV was appropriate for a previous war and whether it was also too heavy for fast-moving expeditionary forces. However, the JLTV's

OCELOT/FOXHOUND LIGHT PROTECTED PATROL VEHICLE (LPPV)

Country of origin: United States/ United Kingdom

Manufacturer: General Dynamics UK/Force Protection Europe

Service: 2011–present

Operator: British Army

Crew: 2, plus 4

Weight: 7500kg (16,535lb)

Dimensions: Length 5.32m (17ft 5in), Width 2.1m (6ft 11in), Height 2.35m (7ft 9in)

Powerplant: Steyr M16 6-cylinder diesel

Range: 500km (310 miles)

Speed: 132km/h (82mph)

Weapons: 2 x 7.62mm (0.3in) machine guns

JOINT LIGHT TACTICAL VEHICLE
US Marine Corps' Joint Light Tactical Vehicles (JLTV) drive to a vehicle staging area, Kingdom of Saudi Arabia.

suite of capabilities, including protection, off-road mobility, modularity and networking, are streets ahead of the Humvee, which it partly replaces.

The armour on the JLTV follows the US Army A kit/B kit principle, whereby the A kit is fitted as standard at the manufacturing stage and the B kit can be added if necessary in the field, according to operational requirements. Two soldiers should be able to fit the B kit in under five hours. Protection includes blast-proof seats. The vehicle also features an automatic fire-extinguishing system. It can operate at temperatures between -40°C and 152C°. It can ford in 152cm (60in) of salt water without a fording kit. The vehicle can be carried on C-130 Hercules and A400M fixed-wing aircraft, as well as underslung on CH-47 Chinook and C53 Sea Stallion helicopters. The JLTV, which has been designed for speed, power and protected mobility, also includes a complete plug-and-play C4ISR capability. Armaments include a roof-mounted 7.62mm (0.3in) or 12.7mm (0.5in) machine gun or a 40mm (1.6in) automatic grenade launcher.

Operations

The JLTV can be used by small units such as special forces on missions that include raids, combat patrols and long-range surveillance.

Arquus SABRE

The Sherpa Light was a family of light armoured vehicles originally developed by Renault Trucks Defense. Unveiled in 2006 and first produced

JOINT LIGHT TACTICAL VEHICLE (JLTV)
Country of origin: United States
Manufacturer: Oshkosh Corporation
Service: 2019–present
Operators: US Army, US Marine Corps
Crew: 4
Weight: 10,200kg (22,500lb)
Dimensions: Length 6.2m (20.5ft), Width 2.5m (8.2ft), Height 2.6m (18.5ft)
Powerplant: Gale Banks Engineering 866T 6.6 litre diesel
Range: 483km (300 miles)
Speed: 110km/h (70mph)
Weapons: N/A

Improvised Explosive Device (IED)

The Improvised Explosive Device (IED), as its name suggests, can be created in a variety of ways and using a wide variety of materials. These include TNT, mortar rounds and even fertilizers. They can be triggered in several ways, either on the command of the attacker or autonomously. Command initiators can be developed from phones, car alarms, remote controls for toys or any other similar systems. Autonomous systems include pressure from vehicles passing over them or magnetic fields.

In terms of attack, the IED may be placed in the path of vehicles or to their sides. It soon became clear to coalition forces that 'traditional' 4x4 vehicles, such as the Land Rover or Humvee, were highly vulnerable to IEDs, even when fitted with armour kits. Only when new vehicles were designed with V-shaped hulls to deflect blasts and much heavier integral armour was it possible for the IED threat against vehicles and their occupants to be neutralized.

From the first Gulf War in 1991 to the War on Terror that began in October 2001, one of the greatest threats to military vehicles used by coalition forces has been the IED. These wars were not the first time that IEDs were used. The Mujahideen had used IEDs against Soviet forces during the Soviet occupation of Afghanistan between 1979 and 1989. They had also been used against the British Army in Northern Ireland from the 1960s to the 1980s. The conflicts in Afghanistan and Iraq, however, saw the most extensive use of the IED and also its greatest influence on vehicle design.

STREET ATTACK
Crowds gather around an Afghan police vehicle damaged by an IED.

in 2007, the Sherpa Light Scout was also manufactured in a badged version by Mack Defense in the USA in 2014. In 2017, Mack Defense revealed the special forces version. French special forces requested a special forces variant, which was initially referred to as the Poids Lourds Forces Speciales (PLFS), or 'Special Forces Heavy Weight'. Once Renault Trucks Defense had come under the ownership of Arquus, the new version of the special forces' vehicle became known as the Sabre.

The Arquus Sabre is designed for use by special forces and elite forces on expeditionary missions that demand high levels of mobility and long range. It replaced the ACMAT VLRA and the Panhard VPS in service with French forces.

The Sabre has an open top and can be adapted to different mission roles and requirements. It has seating for five, including the driver and commander at the front, the gunner in the middle and two at the rear. The front windscreen can be folded down on to the bonnet. It has two front side doors and one door at the rear. The vehicle has armour protection to Level 1 and can be fitted with additional armour for protection against small-arms fire according to mission requirements.

A circular ring mount can be fitted with a 12.7mm (0.5in) FN M2 machine gun and there are also three swivel stations for medium machine guns, one positioned near the commander's door and two at the rear. There are stowage boxes on the left side of the vehicle and a spare wheel on the right side.

ARQUS SABRE
Country of origin: France
Manufacturer: Arquus
Service: 2017–present
Operators: French special forces and paratroopers
Crew: 5
Weight: 11,000kg (24,250lb)
Dimensions: Length 5.43m (17ft 8in), Weight 2.35m (7ft 7in)
Range: 800km (497 miles)
Speed: 110km/h (68mph)
Weapons: 12.7mm (0.5in) heavy machine gun; three medium machine guns (7.62mm (0.3in) or 5.56mm (0.21in))

Arquus Scarab

The Arquus Scarab is a light, protected vehicle with an emphasis on mobility. One of its unique characteristics is the ability to turn both the front and rear axle wheels simultaneously, so that the vehicle can move sideways like a crab. This enables it to emerge rapidly from cover, still forwards, so as to be face-on to the enemy and present a smaller profile. It can then move rapidly back again. The steering system also enables the vehicle to make very tight U-turns, such as when it needs to quickly move out of trouble.

The Scarab carries one driver and three passengers. The driver sits at the front in the centre, giving them 270-degree vision to the front and sides. With a hybrid engine, the Scarab can adopt electric engine mode for silent movement in close proximity to potential danger. The adjustable suspension enables the vehicle to be raised for traversing challenging off-road terrain and lowered when keeping a low profile or when loading on to aircraft. Sliding doors enable crew to access the vehicle while on board an aircraft, where space is restricted. The Scarab can be transported internally by fixed-wing aircraft such as the C-130 or A400M, or by helicopters such as the CH-47 Chinook. It can also be dropped on an LT0012 platform.

Versions

The Scarab is produced in three main versions: the Patrol SAS (PATSAS), with a 12.7mm (0.5in) machine gun; the Reconnaissance, with a 30mm

ARQUUS SCARAB

Country of origin: France

Manufacturer: Arquus (Volvo Group)

Service: N/A

Operators: N/A

Crew: Driver, plus 3

Weight: 8000kg (17,637lb)

Dimensions: Length 5.24m (17ft 2in), Weight 2.1m (6ft 9in), Height 2m (6ft 6in)

Range: N/A

Speed: 130km/h (80mph)

Weapons: 12.7mm (0.5in) machine gun; 40mm (1.6in) grenade launcher; MILAN anti-tank missile; Hornet missile, dependent on configuration and mission

MOWAG EAGLE V
Country of origin: Switzerland
Manufacturer: General
Dynamics Land Systems–Mowag
Service: 2017–present
Operators: German Armed
Forces; Danish Armed Forces;
Swiss Armed Forces; under
consideration by UK armed forces
Crew: Driver, plus 3 or 5
Weight: 16,000kg (35,274lb)
Dimensions: Length 5.4m (17ft
7in), Width 2.3m (7ft 5in), Height
2.3m (7ft 5in)
Powerplant: Cummins 5.9 litre
diesel engine
Range: 650km (400 miles)
Speed: 110km/h (68mph)
Weapons: Browning M2 .50
calibre machine gun; 7.62mm
(0.3in) machine gun; 5.56mm
(0.21in) machine gun; 40mm
automatic grenade launcher

cannon; and the Security, for counter-terrorism and urban operations. The armaments packages may include a small-calibre remote-controlled weapons system (RCWS), a 40mm (1.6in) grenade launcher, a MILAN ATGM or Missile Moyenne Portee (MMP), or a Hornet RCWS. The vehicle also carries smoke-grenade launchers.

The Scarab features the proprietary Arquus battle management system, Battlenet. This provides complete situational awareness, including proximity cameras, vehicle status and weapon status.

MOWAG Eagle V

The Eagle V, like its predecessor the Eagle IV, comes in both 4x4 and 6x6 versions. The main difference between the Eagle V and the Eagle IV is that the newer vehicle has better protection and can also be fitted with modular armour according to mission requirements. The Eagle V has a double V-shaped hull mounted on a DURO chassis and has blast-absorbent seats. The seats can be arranged to accommodate between three and five personnel apart from the driver.

The Eagle V can be augmented with a remotely controlled weapons system that can be fitted with a Browning M2 .50 calibre machine gun, either a 7.62mm (0.3in) or 5.56mm (0.21in) machine gun, or a 40mm (1.6in) grenade launcher. The vehicle can be carried on C-130 and similar sized fixed-wing aircraft, or on a CH-47 Chinook helicopter. The Danish armed forces have ordered the Eagle V in patrol and reconnaissance versions and they are the first armed forces to have ordered the open-top version. Germany deployed Eagle IV vehicles in Afghanistan and, along with Switzerland, uses the Eagle V, too.

LIGHT ALL- TERRAIN VEHICLES

This chapter covers the light, fast attack and reconnaissance vehicles that are so much part of the special forces' DNA. While the previous chapter suggested that special forces had moved towards a more protected type of vehicle, with passive armour shielding the occupants from the IED and ballistic and mine threats that were so much a feature of the wars in Afghanistan and Iraq, here we come full circle to encounter similar vehicles to those featured in Chapter 1, namely adapted Land Rovers or 4x4 Mercedes-Benz vehicles, and the High Mobility Multipurpose Wheeled Vehicle (HMMWV). This may seem contradictory. After all, weren't these vehicles phased out because they did not provide adequate protection for special forces operators and were replaced as a result of urgent operational requirements in both the US and the UK? The answer is that that they were and they weren't, and that the vehicles used depend on mission requirements.

AIRBORNE

The Polaris Deployed Advanced Ground Off-Road (DAGOR) vehicle is typical of the type of ultra-light tactical vehicle designed to move special forces rapidly from the helicopter drop-off point to the objective.

There is still a need for well-protected vehicles that can transport military personnel safely over known routes, and in urban areas where they may be in greater danger of encountering mines and IEDs, or being fired upon from buildings. However, special forces have not relinquished their role in lightning-fast raids in open areas along unpredictable routes in sometimes challenging terrain, often wielding heavy fire power. Such raids will frequently involve insertion into the area by large helicopters such as the CH-47 Chinook or CH-53 Sea Stallion.

Special operations forces are at the cutting edge of innovation and development, seeking always to improve their capabilities in multiple-threat environments. It follows that their equipment must do the same, not least the vehicles that they travel in. So, while the principles of the legacy Jeeps, Land Rovers and other similar vehicles remain the same, many of the vehicles described in this chapter have been specifically developed to set new standards in off-road capability and mobility across challenging terrain, in carrying increased payloads while being light enough for easy airlift, and incorporating greater modularity so that they can be adapted quickly according to mission requirements. Advances in independent suspension, along with ride-height adjustment, are linked to powerful engines and the capability for long ranges. Passive armour is usually minimal to preserve agility, but can often be added according to mission requirements. Vehicles come in various layouts for either two or four or more operators, or can be adapted by adding extra seats. Typically, a heavy weapon such as a .50 calibre machine gun or 40mm (1.6in) automatic

ALL-TERRAIN VEHICLE
Soldiers with Special Operations Task Force – South prepare to load an all-terrain vehicle on to a CH-47 Chinook helicopter in preparation for a rapid offload during operations in the Maruf District, Kandahar Province, Afghanistan.

grenade launcher will be mounted on a central 360° ring mount, while swing arm mounts can be fitted with medium 7.62mm (0.3in) or light 5.56mm (0.21in) machine guns.

Air transport is another vital factor in the design and development of light all-terrain vehicles. Special forces and elite units often rely on transport to the mission drop-off area by large helicopters such as the Ch-47 Chinook or CH-53 Sea Stallion, or by the tiltrotor CV-22 Osprey, or by fixed-wing aircraft such as the C-130 Hercules or A400M. The challenge for designers of light all-terrain vehicles (LATVs) is to create a vehicle that can either be carried internally and/or underslung while also having the capacity to carry personnel and their equipment and armaments, as well as the robustness to tackle challenging terrain on route to the target area. A good example of minimalist design is the Polaris Government and Defense MRZR Alpha, which is the latest iteration in the successful MRZR range and which incorporates greater space and better off-road mobility in a highly compact package. Special forces operators are trained to travel light and the MRZR Alpha mirrors that principle.

POLARIS MRZR D2

US Marines with 3rd Marine Division load an MRZR lightweight tactical all-terrain vehicle onboard a KC-130 Hercules aircraft during Assault Support Tactics 4, as part of Weapons and Tactics Instructors Course 1-19 at Forward Operating Base Laguna, US Army Yuma Proving Grounds, Arizona.

S-ATV Special Purpose All-Terrain Vehicle

First unveiled in 2012, the Oshkosh S-ATV was designed for special operations and was a contender for the US Special Operations Command GMV1.1 Ground Mobility Vehicle competition, which was eventually won by General Dynamics with its Flyer 70 vehicle.

**S-ATV SPECIAL PURPOSE
ALL-TERRAIN VEHICLE**
Country of origin: United States
Manufacturer: Oshkosh
Service: N/A
Operators: N/A
Crew: N/T
Weight: 3740kg (8245lb)
Dimensions: Length 5m (16ft
5in), Width 2m (6ft 6in)
Powerplant: 6.6 litre Duramax
VG diesel
Range: 800km (500 miles)
Speed: 145km/h (90mph)
Weapons: 12.7mm (0.5in)
machine gun; 7.62mm (0.3in)
machine guns

The S-ATV is a modular design that can be used for search and rescue (SAR), reconnaissance, rapid response and counter-insurgency operations. It has a standard box design with the engine at the front, crew in the middle and storage space at the rear. There is a roll-over bar for added crew safety in rough terrain. Armour protection can be added or removed according to mission requirements. The S-ATV is fitted with two doors and has a three-piece windshield. The cargo compartment can be used to carry spare weapons, ammunition, fuel, water and other supplies. The vehicle can carry five personnel as standard, including the driver and gunner, or it can be extended to carry seven personnel. Powered by a V8 diesel engine linked to an Allison automatic transmission, the S-ATV can achieve considerable ranges for extended missions while also having enough speed to get out of trouble. Off-road mobility is enhanced by the TAK 4i independent suspension, while the central tyre inflation system enables optimum traction according to the terrain.

The main armament is fitted to a 360-degree weapon ring that can accommodate a range of arms, including a 12.7mm (0.5in) or 7.62mm (0.3in) machine gun. There is also a weapon station fixed to the side of the vehicle. The vehicle has plug and play command, control, communications, communications and intelligence (C4I) capability.

The S-ATV is compact enough to be carried in a range of fixed-wing aircraft, as well as the CH-47 Chinook and CH-53 Sea Stallion helicopters.

Desert Patrol Vehicle (DPV)

The Desert Patrol Vehicle (DPV) was an innovative design that was developed in the 1980s for a general military role but which soon came to be used as a long-range reconnaissance vehicle for special forces. With

DESERT PATROL VEHICLE

Country of origin: United States

Manufacturer: Chenoweth Racing Products Inc.

Service: 1991–present

Operators: US Navy SEALs

Crew: 3

Weight: 957kg (2110lb)

Dimensions: Length 4.08m (13ft 4in), Width 2.11m (6ft 9in), Height 2.01m (6ft 6in)

Powerplant: 2 ltire VW air-cooled

Range: 320km (200 miles)

Speed: 47km/h (60mph)

Weapons: M2 Browning .50 calibre machine gun; 2 x M60 7.62mm (0.3in) machine guns; 2x M136 AT4 anti-armour weapons; Mk 19 40mm (1.6in) grenade launcher; M240 machine gun; M249 SAW

its powerful air-cooled VW engine and trailing-arm suspension and shock absorbers, the DPV could move fast across rugged terrain. It was also designed to mount a variety of both heavy and light weaponry, including .50 calibre machine guns, grenade launchers, and medium or light machine guns.

It was deployed by US Navy SEALs in Operation Desert Storm, when they were the first coalition vehicles to enter Kuwait City after it was liberated from Saddam Hussein's Iraqi forces. The DPVs were able to avoid the roads that had been booby trapped by the retreating Iraqis.

The DPV was also deployed by Special Forces Operational Detachment-Delta (SFOD-Delta) in the same conflict.

M1161 Growler Internally Transportable Light Strike Vehicle

Designed specifically to fit in the V-22 Osprey, the M1161 Growler replaced the much larger Mercedes-Benz Interim Fast Attack Vehicle (IFAV). Designed for light utility, light strike and fast attack, the M1161 Growler is one of the smallest vehicles in its class.

DESERT PATROL VEHICLE
US Navy SEALs drive a desert patrol vehicle. The design and configuration of the DPV seem somewhat basic compared to the light tactical all-terrain vehicles now available to special forces.

M1161 GROWLER

US Marines reconnaissance forces in an M1161
Internally Transportable Vehicle during a training
exercise at Camp Pendleton, California, 2015.

M1161 GROWLER
Country of origin: United States
Manufacturer: General
Dynamics
Service: 2009–present
Operators: US Marine Corps
Marine Expeditionary Units
(MEUs)
Crew: Driver, plus 3
Weight: 2058kg (4537lb)
Dimensions: Length 4.14m (13ft
6in), Width 1.5m (4ft 9in), Height
1.19m (3ft 9in)
Powerplant: 2.8 litre 4-cylinder
turbo-diesel
Range: 657km (408 miles)
Speed: 137km/h (85mph)
Weapons: M2 .50 calibre
Browning machine gun;
Mk 19 40mm (1.6in) automatic
grenade launcher

The M1161 Growler was ordered by US Marine Corps Systems Command (MCSC) in November 2004 and, after several delays in development, it was deployed by US Marine Expeditionary Units (MEUs) in January 2009. Although intended for infantry use, due to its size limitations the M1161 Growler was mostly deployed by special operations units for reconnaissance and light strike missions. It was also used as a logistics and medical vehicle, and could be fitted with a system that allowed the vehicle to be operated remotely.

Like most vehicles of its type, the M1161 Growler had limited armour protection, relying instead on speed and agility to keep out of harm's way. Having seen limited action with the Marine Corps, the M1161 Growler is due to be replaced. Reports suggest that it will not be missed.

Polaris MRZR D2 and D4 Light Tactical Military Vehicles
The MRZR vehicles are fast, light and highly mobile, providing expeditionary forces with the ability to tackle challenging off-road terrain to achieve their objectives. The vehicles come in various forms, including petrol and diesel, with capacity ranging from two to six personnel, depending on the version. Designed to be deployed in forward areas, the vehicles can carry troops along with their essential equipment, along with enough armament for defence and attack.

Although they lack armour protection, the MRZR vehicles use speed and off-road mobility to evade enemy contact when necessary, though the vehicles can also be used for lightning raids. They can travel over terrain that would not be accessible to larger vehicles. Roll-over bars provide protection for the crew, and they can be easily folded when the vehicle is loaded into an aircraft.

There is a small cargo area at the rear of the vehicle that can be adapted in various ways, either to carry equipment and supplies, such as spare fuel and water, or to be used for stretchers. It can also carry extra crew if necessary on two rear-facing seats. If more carrying capacity is needed, a special off-road trailer can be towed, adding 454kg (1000lb) of capacity.

The petrol versions are powered by a three-cylinder Polaris ProStar 900 petrol engine. The diesel version is powered by a Kohler turbo-diesel engine. The MRZR features a system whereby the standard two-wheel drive can switch automatically to four-wheel drive when extra traction is required. The transmission is automatic and continuously variable. Power steering reduces driver strain in rough terrain. The vehicles are fitted with independent dual A-arm suspension at the front and independent trailing arms at the rear.

The vehicles can be fitted with 5.56mm (0.21in) or 7.62mm (0.3in) machine guns or with a 40mm (1.6in) grenade launcher for either defence or attack. The open structure allows crew to use their personal weapons for defence or assault. An infrared (IR) light can be used when driving in black-out mode at night. The vehicle can also be fitted with durable MOLLE-coated roof panels for overhead protection from the elements.

MRZR D2 & D4
Country of origin: United States
Manufacturer: Polaris
Government and Defense
Service: 2016–present
Operators: US Special Operations
Command (USSOCOM); US
Marine Corps
Crew: 5–7
Weight: D2 856kg (1887lb);
D4 952.54kg (2100lb)
Dimensions: D2 Length 2.87m
(9ft 7in), Width 1.51m (4ft 9in),
Height 1.87m (6ft 1in); D4 Length
3.56m (11ft 7in), Width 1.51m
(4ft 9in), Height 187m (6ft 1in)
Powerplant: 4-stroke SOHC
3-cylinder turbo-diesel
Range: 250km (155 miles)
Speed: 96km/h (60mph)
Weapons: Personal weapons
used by crew

MRZR D2
The MRZR D2 is a model of compact design, providing special forces with mobility along with easy transportation of their essential equipment.

CV-22 Osprey

Some of the vehicles in this chapter, and the M1161 Growler in particular, have been designed for transport in the limited space of the CV-22 Osprey tiltrotor aircraft. The CV-22 is the US Air Force Special Operations Command version of the V-22 Osprey aircraft. The US Marine Corps version is the MV-22. The world's first and only tiltrotor aircraft, the Osprey achieves the best of both worlds between the operational range and speed of a conventional fixed-wing aircraft and the vertical lift and hover advantages of a helicopter.

The US Air Force says that 'the mission of CV-22 is to conduct long-range infiltration, exfiltration and resupply missions for special operations forces', and it can 'perform missions that normally would require both fixed-wing and rotary wing aircraft'.

Features of the CV-22 include integrated threat countermeasures, terrain-following radar and forward-looking infrared sensors, along with a variety of other systems that enable it to operate successfully in high-threat environments. Special operations features in the cockpit also include night-vision goggle compatible displays and integrated helmet displays.

A 7.62mm (0.3in) machine gun is mounted near the rear ramp and a remotely operated turret is under development by BAE Systems.

The CV-22 can carry 24 combat-ready special forces operators and these can be dropped by the FAST rope system from a hover position if necessary. It can also carry a light all-terrain vehicle for rapid deployment off the back ramp after landing.

AIR MOBILE
Soldiers assigned to 10th Special Forces Group (Airborne) load a MRZR ultra-light ground mobility vehicle on to a US Air Force CV-22 Osprey during air infiltration training on Hurlburt Field, Florida, 2016.

Polaris MRZR Alpha LTATV

The Polaris Alpha LTATV was the latest version of their successful MRZR series of light tactical and all-terrain vehicles and it was officially unveiled at the Defence and Security Equipment International exhibition in London in September 2021. However, by then the Alpha had already been delivered to the United States Special Operations Command (USSOCOM) and US Marine Corps under the US Light Tactical All-Terrain Vehicle (LTATV) and Ultra-Light Tactical Vehicle (ULTV) programmes.

One might ask how such a minimalist and compact vehicle as the MRZR could be significantly improved, given that it already does a good job of carrying between two and four personnel and their equipment over challenging terrain.

Although not immediately obvious to the eye, Polaris have made several changes and improvements. A new and more durable chassis provides scope for greater loads, more room for personnel and greater flexibility with cargo loads than previous versions. The Alpha also has higher ground clearance overall and incorporates high-clearance front and rear dual-arm suspension. The innovative suspension system ensures that the Alpha's ride height can be maintained even when the vehicle is fully loaded. The ground clearance can also be raised from 30cm to 36cm (12in to 14in), depending on the terrain. The powerful common rail turbo-diesel engine is linked to a high performance eight-speed transmission.

The Alpha can be transported in the holds of the tiltrotor V-22 Osprey as well as CH-47 Chinook and CH-53 Sea Stallion helicopters. It can also be

MRZR D4
The MRZR D4 is a compact air-portable all-terrain vehicle which can transport four soldiers and their personal equipment over harsh off-road terrain.

POLARIS ALPHA LTATV
Country of origin: United States
Manufacturer: Polaris
Government and Defense
Service: 2021–present
Operators: United States
Special Operations Command
(USSOCOM); US Marine Corps
Crew: 2/4
Weight: N/A
Dimensions: N/A
Powerplant: Common rail turbo
diesel
Range: 362km (225 miles)
Speed: 96km/h (60mph)
Weapons: Personal weapons
used by crew

carried as a slung load. In addition, it can be delivered by the Low Velocity Air Drop (LVAD) and Joint P Airdrop (JPAD) systems.

Other technical advances featured in the Alpha are high-energy laser systems, intelligence, surveillance and reconnaissance systems, a tactical aviation ground refuelling system, expeditionary command and control systems, and a variety of communications equipment.

Flyer Ground Mobility Vehicle 1.1

In 2012 United States Special Operations Command (USSOCOM) issued a requirement for a vehicle that would replace its fleet of Humvee-based ground mobility vehicles. The brief stated that the new vehicle should have significantly greater mobility capabilities than the HMMWV as well as being able to support the latest generation C4ISR electronics, and provide additional firepower. The new vehicle would need to be transportable by air and capable of carrying out a variety of missions, including light strike, reconnaissance, personnel rescue and recovery and communications.

In August 2013, General Dynamics, working with Flyer Defense, was announced as the winner of the GMV1.1 competition and the initial contract was for 1300 vehicles. In 2017, there was an additional SOCOM order for 300 vehicles in a nine-passenger GMV configuration to support the five airborne infantry brigade combat teams.

To design a vehicle that could move rapidly over rough terrain, carrying personnel, their equipment, armaments and ammunition required good ground clearance, significant allowance for approach and departure angles, and robust suspension. The Flyer GMV1.1 comes with a modular armour kit that can be fitted for relevant missions and protection to ballistic level B6.

In January 2018, SOCOM awarded a contract for a heavy-duty turret to be retrofitted to Flyer vehicles to provide additional protection to the gunner.

The Flyer GMV1.1 was also under consideration by UK Special Forces (UKSF) under Operation Westerly, the project to identify a light strike vehicle for UK special forces.

Flyer 60

The Flyer 60 Internally Transportable Vehicle is a narrower version of the Flyer 72, which is designed for maximum air transportability in aircraft such as the V-22 Osprey, CH-53 Stallion and CH-130 Hercules. The Flyer 60 is available in several variants, adapted to specific missions such as rescue and personnel recovery, reconnaissance, light strike with or without armour, C4ISR and communications. Due to its smaller size, the Flyer 60 is better equipped for rapid evasive manoeuvrability and confined spaces.

Polaris Dagor A1

The Dagor (Deployable Advanced Ground Off-Road Vehicle) A1 is an ultra-light combat vehicle which is designed to quickly transport special forces and light infantry to their objectives across challenging terrain. Despite its relatively light weight, the Dagor A1 can transport up to nine military personnel and their essential equipment, as well as deploying a selection of armaments according to force and mission requirements. The vehicle is compact enough to be carried in the hold of a CH-47 Chinook or CH-53 Sea Stallion helicopter, as well as a range of fixed-wing aircraft. It can also be delivered via the Low Velocity Air Drop (LVAD) system.

FLYER DEFENSE
Country of origin: United States
Manufacturer: General Dynamics/ Flyer Defense
Service: 2020–present
Operators: United States Special Operations Command (USSOCOM)
Crew: Flyer 72, 9; Flyer 60, 4
Weight: Flyer 72, 2495kg (3500lb); Flyer 60, 2041kg (4500lb)
Dimensions: Flyer 72 Length 4.6m (15ft 1in), Width 1.8m (6ft); Flyer 60 Length 4.57m (15ft), Height 1.52m (5ft)
Powerplant: 2 litre direct injection GM DOHC turbocharged intercoooled JP8 diesel
Range: Flyer 72, 483km (300 miles); Flyer 60, 563km (350 miles)
Speed: 153 km/h (95mph)
Weapons: 360 foldable turret; M2 .50 calibre machine gun; 7.62mm (0.3in) machine gun; GAU 19; 5.56mm (0.21in) and 7.62mm (0.3in) swing-arm mounts

With its rugged, modular design, the Dagor A1 also incorporates commercial off-the-shelf (COTS) components, making for ease of maintenance and availability of spare parts. It is also powered by a commercial turbo-diesel JP8 engine along with electronic power steering and intuitive control systems.

The diesel engine provides better mission adaptability, as it can use fuel that is more widely available than refined petrol. Diesel engines also provide more torque for demanding travel over rugged terrain with substantial loads. Customers can request additional equipment and accessories according to their service and operational needs. The vehicle is designed to be easily maintained.

The three-box design allows room for personnel as well as equipment in the rear. Where a full complement of personnel is required, four can be seated in the rear area with items such as rucksacks hung on the outside of the vehicle. There is a sling seat hung from the roof bar for the gunner. Alternatively, the rear storage area can be used to carry spare equipment, including ammunition, spare fuel and water, and other supplies. The open-door design allows personnel to use their personal weapons and to deploy quickly from the vehicle. The weapons ring can be adapted to fit up to 48 different kinds of weaponry and there are pintle mounts for machine guns.

The Dagor A1 was a contender for the Ground Mobility Vehicle GMV1.1 contest, which was won by General Dynamics and Flyer Defense with their Flyer 72. However, the story does not end there, as interest in the Dagor continues both in the US and abroad. The Canadian Special Operations Forces Command (CANSOFCOM) ordered several Dagor vehicles to fulfil its Ultra-Light Combat Vehicle (ULCV) requirement and the Dagor vehicles were delivered with tailored equipment packages.

POLARIS DAGOR A1

Country of origin: United States

Manufacturer: Polaris Government and Defense Dagor A1

Service: N/A

Operators: Canadian Special Operations Forces Command (CANSOFCOM)

Crew: 9

Weight: 3856kg (8500lb)

Dimensions: Length 4.5m (14ft 8in), Width 1.88m (6ft 2in)

Powerplant: JP8 turbo-diesel engine

Range: 805km (500 miles)

Speed: Not known

Weapons: .50 calibre heavy machine gun

POLARIS DAGOR A1
The Polaris Dagor can carry up to nine personnel and their personal equipment, four facing forwards and four in the rear compartment facing inwards. Alternatively, it can carry four personnel as well as essential supplies and equipment.

Boeing Phantom Badger

Developed on the request of the US Special Operations community, the Boeing Phantom Badger was designed as a compact and mobile vehicle that could move fast over challenging terrain after delivery by fixed-wing aircraft or helicopter. The Badger was officially cleared by the US Navy for use in the V-22 Osprey tiltrotor aircraft, making it part of a select group that can be transported in the internal holds of not only the Osprey but the CH-47 Chinook and CH-53 Sea Stallion helicopters.

The Badger was developed by Boeing with significant input from the small company MSI, which was responsible for designing the shocks and suspension system in order to withstand the rough rides that the vehicle would be likely to encounter during special forces operations. The suspension can be raised for more challenging terrain, and it can ford water 1m (3ft) deep, and the four-wheel steering system allows the vehicle to turn within a 7.3m (24ft) radius.

Another aspect of the Badger is its modularity. It has mission-specific rear modules that can be changed in the field in under 30 minutes, according to mission requirements. This means that the Badger can be adapted to missions that include reconnaissance, combat search and rescue, casualty transport and explosive ordnance disposal. The Badger can carry five personnel, including the driver and front passenger, with one person sitting in the middle and two at the rear seated in detachable rear-facing seats.

Apart from the specially designed suspension system, the Badger is manufactured from commercial off-the-shelf components and its V6 3-litre turbo-diesel engine is taken from the Jeep Grand Cherokee.

Supacat Light Reconnaissance Vehicle (LRV 400)

First unveiled in London in 2013, the Supacat LRV 400 is a high-speed, high-mobility vehicle designed for special forces and reconnaissance units.

BOEING PHANTOM BADGER

Country of origin: United States
Manufacturer: Boeing/MSI Defence Systems
Service: 2014–present
Operators: US Navy; US Marine Corps
Crew: 5
Weight: 3402kg (7850lb)
Dimensions: Length 4.57m (14ft 10in), Width 1.5m (4ft 9in)
Powerplant: 240 bhp multi-fuel engine
Range: 724km (450 miles)
Speed: 128km/h (80mph)
Weapons: 12.7mm (0.5in) machine gun; 7.62mm (0.3in) machine guns; 40mm (1.6in) automatic grenade launcher

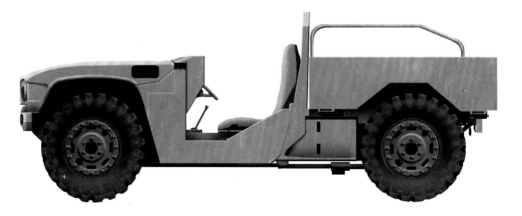

Based on the Land Rover Discovery 4 chassis and inspired by the Wildcat off-road motorsport vehicle, the LRV 400 is compact enough to be carried inside a CH-47 Chinook helicopter, giving it an advantage over the HMT 400 vehicle already in service with UK special forces.

Supacat worked with the motorsport company, QT Services, which was responsible for developing the shock absorbers and suspension system. The chassis was also strengthened so that it could carry a military load, including spare fuel, water and other supplies, as well as armaments. With its Land Rover heritage, the obvious comparison is with the Desert Patrol Vehicle (DPV) used by British special forces in the Gulf War.

So far as protection is concerned, the LRV 400 features specially designed seats by ArmourWorks. Its low-weight armour package can be augmented according to mission requirements.

The LRV 400 comes with a load of extras designed to maximize mission effectiveness, including run-flat tyres, infrared (IR) lights, forward and rear-facing IR cameras and LED high-input T16 driving lights. There are also options for grenade launchers, a remote weapons station and other weapon mounts. An onboard jacking system allows the vehicle to be lifted when grounded. Communications equipment can also be added according to customer requirements.

The LRV 400 was a contender in the Operation Westerly project, as was the Flyer 72.

SUPACAT LIGHT RECONNAISSANCE VEHICLE LRV-400

Country of origin: United Kingdom
Manufacturer: Supacat
Service: N/A
Operators: N/A
Crew: 3
Weight: 4200kg (9478lb)
Dimensions: Length 4.6m (15ft 1in), Width 1.7m (5ft 6in), Height 1.80m (5ft 9in)
Powerplant: 3.2 litre diesel
Range: 800km (497 miles)
Speed: 160km/h (99mph)
Weapons: 12.7mm (0.5in) machine gun; 7.62mm (0.3in) machine gun; 40mm (1.6in) grenade launcher

P6 ALL-TERRAIN ASSAULT VEHICLE (ATAV)

Country of origin: Indonesia
Manufacturer: SSE Defense
Service: 2016–present
Operators: Indonesian special forces; Indonesian Marines
Crew: 5
Weight: 2.3 tonnes (2.5 tons)
Dimensions: Length 4.6m (15ft 1in), Width 2.3m (7ft 5in), Height 1.5m (4ft 9in)
Powerplant: 4-cylinder turbo-diesel 2.3-litre 142 HP
Range: 500km (311 miles)
Speed: 120km/h (75mph)
Weapons: 12.7mm (0.5in) machine gun; 7.62mm (0.3in) machine gun

P6 All-Terrain Assault Vehicle (ATAV)

This highly mobile reconnaissance, support and assault vehicle was designed for Indonesian special forces, and other arms of the Indonesian military, and was first introduced in 2016. Manufactured by SSE Defense, the P6 has a tubular frame open-body design, allowing for ease of movement for special forces operators, as well as the use of personal weapons. The vehicle is manufactured from a mixture of steel and aluminium and in its open-top form has minimal armour protection.

The P6 can carry five operators, including the driver and commander at the front, two at the rear and a gunner in a raised position at the centre. Powered by a 4-cylinder 2.3-litre turbo-diesel engine, the P6 has independent suspension designed to provide good mobility over challenging terrain. Equipment includes run-flat tyres and a gunshot detection system.

There is an enclosed, armoured version of the P6 called the V3 which provides Level 1 STANAG ballistic protection, including bullet-proof windows at the front. This version can be fitted with a remote-control weapon system (RCWS) mounting either a 12.7mm (0.5in) or 7.62mm (0.3in) machine gun. The V3 version is in service with Indonesian air force special forces – the Korps Pasukan Khas (or Paskhas). The Indonesian navy marines also operate versions of the P6.

KMW Special Operations Vehicle (SOV)

In 2000, German special forces requested a light long-range reconnaissance vehicle that could also be airlifted in a CH-47 Chinook helicopter. Krauss-Maffei Wegman worked with the Italian firm Bremach to build a vehicle around a Bremach chassis. The vehicle is open-topped and lightly armoured with the crew seating set high in order to provide greater protection against mines or IEDs. With an easily foldable roll-bar, the vehicle can be transported in the hold of a CH-47 Chinook or CH-53 Sea Stallion helicopter, or by C-130 Hercules and A400M fixed-wing aircraft.

The modular design of the SOV allows for the development of different mission variants. The SOV is equipped with three mounts which can be fitted with a variety of weapons, including a 12.7mm (0.5in) heavy machine gun or a 40mm (1.6in) automatic grenade launcher on the main ring mount. Two pedestal mounts can be fitted with either 7.62mm (0.3in) general purpose machine guns or 5.56mm (0.21in) light machine guns. The SOV can also be fitted with a smoke grenade launcher.

Integrated Convoy Protection (ICP) REVA FAV

The REVA FAV was designed by ex-special forces operators for active special forces operators. It is intended for raids, search and rescue, and reconnaissance. In the tradition of David Stirling's SAS Jeeps that operated in the North African desert during World War II, the FAV is designed to be fast and effective, relying on its speed and mobility for protection rather than on passive armour.

However, on the basis that special operations vehicles of this type are more likely to meet their opponents head-on, the FAV has armour protection as standard on the front and on the sides of the engine

KMW SPECIAL OPERATIONS VEHICLE (SOV)
Country of origin: Germany
Manufacturer: Krauss-Maffei Wegman/Bremach
Service: 2014–present
Operators: German special forces
Crew: 6
Weight: 4.5 tonnes (5 tons)
Dimensions: Length 5.99m (19ft 6in), Width 1.94m (6ft 4in), Height 2.63m (8ft 6in)
Powerplant: IVECO 3 litre diesel engine
Range: 900km (559 miles)
Speed: 130km/h (81mph)
Weapons: 12.7mm (0.5in) machine gun; 7.62mm (0.3in) machine gun; 5.56mm (0.21in) machine gun; 40mm automatic machine gun

compartment. It is also fitted with a belly plate. Additional armour can be fitted, namely door panels and a rear bay canopy, for Level B6 ballistic protection, but this compromises the speed and agility of the vehicle. The FAV is designed to protect itself through speed, mobility, surprise and firepower.

The rugged suspension handles rapid movement over challenging terrain from the drop-off area (the FAV can be carried in a CH-47 Chinook helicopter or underslung) to the point of contact using unpredictable routes to avoid mines and IEDs.

Apart from the commander and driver, the FAV can seat four at the rear with the option to add extra seats. A mini turret can be mounted with a .50 calibre machine gun, 40mm (1.6in) automatic grenade launcher or 60mm (2.4in) mortar. Swing arms on the side next to the commander and driver can be fitted with either 7.62mm (0.3in) or 5.56mm (0.21in) machine guns. The FAV is also fitted with a winch and a central tyre inflation system.

Like other REVA vehicles, the FAV has been proven in several different challenging environments, from deserts to tropical jungles. It has been used by special forces in Iraq as well as in Thailand.

NIMR Automotive Rapid Intervention Vehicle (RIV)

Developed by NIMR Automotive in the United Arab Emirates with significant engineering and design input from UK-based MIRA, the RIV was developed for armed reconnaissance and covert special operations over long ranges and in extreme temperatures.

ICP REVA FAV
Country of origin: South Africa
Manufacturer: Integrated Convoy Protection (ICP)
Service: N/A
Operators: US, Iraqi and Thai special forces
Crew: 6
Weight: N/A
Dimensions: N/A
Powerplant: Cummins 3.8 litre turbo-diesel
Range: 840km (522 miles)
Speed: 150km/h (93mph)
Weapons: .50 calibre machine gun; 40mm (1.6in) automatic grenade launcher; 7.62mm (0.3in) machine gun; 5.56mm (0.21in) machine gun

NIMR AUTOMOTIVE RAPID INTERVENTION VEHICLE (RIV)

Country of origin: United Arab Emirates

Manufacturer: NIMR Automotive/ MIRA

Service: N/A

Operators: United Arab Emirates armed forces

Crew: 4

Weight: 4000kg (8818lb)

Dimensions: Length 8.9m (29ft 2in), Width 2m (6ft 6in), Height 1.81m (5ft 9in)

Powerplant: 300hp diesel engine

Range: 1000km (621 miles)

Speed: 160km/h (99mph)

Weapons: 12.7mm (0.5in) machine gun; 7.62mm (0.3in) machine gun; 5.56mm (0.21in) machine gun

Like many vehicles of its type, the RIV relies on speed and mobility for protection rather than passive armour. It is fitted with a blast-protective belly plate and additional appliqué armour can be added on request, depending on mission requirements.

The lightweight design includes a roll-cage frame. The RIV can be carried inside a CH-47 Chinook helicopter or can be underslung. It can tackle a wide range of terrain, including hard and soft sandy areas in deserts or, in more northern areas, soft, muddy conditions. A central tyre inflation system can be used to maximize traction according to the terrain.

One of the major characteristics of the RIV is its ability to operate in extreme temperatures such as those found in desert environments, where extreme heat in the day can transition to extreme cold at night. A 'winterized' version of the RIV has also been developed so that the vehicle can operate successfully in the colder and wetter conditions of Eastern Europe.

Optional equipment includes a battery management system, add-on ballistic protection, run-flat inserts, C4I command and control, and ride-height control for challenging terrain.

The RIV can centrally mount a 12.7mm (0.5in) heavy machine gun or 7.62mm (0.3in) or 5.56mm (0.21in) machine guns on the sides.

The RIV is another example of a vehicle that has been developed to provide fast intervention with the ability to transition quickly from the back of a helicopter and take overland routes to its target, maximizing surprise and firepower.

SPIDER LSV II

Country of origin: Singapore

Manufacturer: ST Kinetics

Service: 2013–present

Operators: Singapore special
forces

Crew: 4

Weight: 1600kg (3527lbs)

Dimensions: Length 4.5m (14ft
8in), Width 2.03m (6ft 7in)

Powerplant: Peugeot 4-cylinder
2.8 litre engine

Range: 800km/h (500 miles)

Speed: 120km/h (75mph)

Weapons: 12.7mm (0.5in)
machine gun; 7.62mm (0.3in)
machine gun; 5.56mm (0.21in)
machine gun; optional 120mm
(4.7in) mortar

Zetor Engineering Fox Rapid Deployment Vehicle (RDV)

The Fox Rapid Deployment Vehicle is used in a Mercedes-Benz G300 CDI chassis. Designed for the rapid deployment of special forces, the Fox has good off-road performance and can carry four crew members along with their equipment and armaments. The Fox is designed to be modular and adaptable, according to mission requirements. Apart from the four seats for the driver, commander and two passengers, there is a fifth seat at the rear for a gunner. There is a mechanical turret located in the roof that can be fitted with a 12.7mm (0.5in) heavy machine gun and swing arms on the sides of the vehicle can be fitted with four 7.62mm (0.3in) or 5.56mm (0.21in) machine guns. The turret can also be fitted with a launcher for an anti-tank guided missile (ATGM).

Spider Light Strike Vehicle II

Designed for strike and reconnaissance missions, as well as scouting and low-intensity guerrilla warfare, the Spider Light Strike II vehicle is a fully revised version of the original Spider Light Strike vehicle. Developed by ST Kinetics and operational with Singapore special forces from 2013, the LSV II is light, fast and easily transportable by helicopter. The new version includes navigation and positioning technology, and an integrated automatic fire control system. It can be equipped with lightweight composite armour around the cabin area in order to provide ballistic and fragment protection. The LSV II has double wishbone front suspension and trailing arm rear suspension. It has hydraulic power-assisted steering and power-assisted ABS brakes.

Koluman Otomotiv Industri LSA4

This rugged 4x4 open-top vehicle has been developed by the Turkish manufacturer Koluman to support light strike, reconnaissance and support missions. Like many vehicles of its type, it has been designed to be light and compact enough to be carried by air or sea for rapid deployment. Its modular design allows the vehicle to be rapidly reconfigured, depending on mission requirements. This includes the addition of a hard-top for increased crew protection in high-threat areas.

The LSA4 is fitted with baseline armour protection to STANAG 1 and also features an integrated mine protection kit.

The LSA4 is powered by a Ford 5-cylinder common rail turbo-diesel engine linked to a ZF automatic six-speed transmission. It has solid beam suspension with floating axles and trailing arms. It is fitted with long-travel shock absorbers and roll stabilizers. The vehicle also features a roll-bar and self-recovery winch for when the terrain becomes particularly tough.

Armament includes a .50 calibre machine gun mounted on the roof and there is a swing-arm mount for either a 7.62mm (0.3in) or 5.56mm (0.21in) machine gun. Electrically powered smoke grenade launchers are positioned at all four corners of the vehicle.

KOLUMAN OTOMOTIV INDUSTRI LSA4

Country of origin: Turkey
Manufacturer: Koluman Otomotiv Industri
Service: N/A
Operators: Turkish armed forces
Crew: 4
Weight: 2310kg (5093lb)
Dimensions: 5.1m (16ft 7in), Width 1.8m (5ft 9in), Height 1.8m (5ft 9in)
Powerplant: Ford 5-cylinder common rail turbo-diesel
Range: 800km (497 miles)
Speed: 140kmh (86 miles)
Weapons: .50 calibre machine gun; 7.62mm (0.3in) or 5.56mm (0.21in) machine gun

SUPPORT VEHICLES

Although not as exotic or spectacular as the lighter and faster special forces tactical vehicles, support vehicles nevertheless have often made an essential contribution to mission success.The Long Range Desert Group in World War II carried out long-range reconnaissance missions that meant that they were far from any sources of supply. To resolve the supply problem, some of the Chevrolet or Ford 30cwt vehicles were allocated to a supply troop and carried spare equipment and supplies for extended periods of operation. This allowed other vehicles with armaments to travel lighter and to be available for attack or defence. In due course, even heavier trucks were allocated to supply duties, including Marmion-Herrington trucks that were used for logistical support, transporting supplies such as fuel, ammunition, water, rations, camouflage nets and spare tyres.

VLRA
The VLRA light tactical vehicle is purpose-built as a military vehicle and is extremely robust. VLRA support vehicles are trusted by special forces worldwide.

UNIMOG U-4000

The Mercedes Unimog is a reliable go-anywhere supply and support vehicle. High portal axles and all-wheel drive give it exceptional ground clearance.

Fifty years later, during the First Gulf War, the SAS found itself in similar operational circumstances. Having been designated along with 1st Special Forces Operational Detachment-Delta (1st SFOD-Delta) to monitor and search the Iraqi desert for Scud ballistic missile launchers that were being aimed at Israel, D Squadron SAS drove into Iraq from Saudi Arabia in eight heavily-armed Land Rover 110s, accompanied by Unimog support vehicles. In a similar way to the Long Range Desert Group, the SAS carried out road-watch missions to intercept relevant Iraqi vehicles, as well as other patrols. The support vehicles enabled them to carry out longer patrols than would otherwise have been the case. Supplies were supplemented by RAF 47 Squadron CH-47 Chinooks, and eventually a major resupply effort was organized whereby British Army four-ton trucks escorted by armed Land Rover 90 'Dinkies' drove from Saudi Arabia, penetrating about 160km (100 miles) into the Iraqi desert where they had a rendezvous with SAS patrol units at a wadi complex.

Delta Force had infiltrated into its sector of 'Scud Alley' in various ways, including air insertion by the 160th Special Operations Aviation Regiment (160th SOAR) and US Air Force Special Operations Command (AFSOC) MH-53J Pavelow III helicopters. Other Delta Force units drove across the Saudi Arabian border in adapted HMMWVs, accompanied by Fast Attack vehicles and motorcycles.

Similar operations were repeated in the Iraq War in 2003, when special forces from the United States, the United Kingdom and Australia were deployed to attack or secure significant Iraqi targets, including missile bases, communications centres, dams and airfields. However, having learned from their experience in the first Gulf War, Iraqi forces sent out patrols to intercept Allied special forces, resulting in several confrontations. The same requirement for support vehicles applied in this conflict as in the previous one.

As special forces continued to engage in operations in Afghanistan, and as new vehicles were developed, the same principles applied. The manufacturer Supacat came up with the ingenious solution of lengthening a 4x4 vehicle to a 6x6 vehicle, thereby increasing payload and capacity.

Arquus VLRA-2

The Arquus VLRA-2 is a development of the VLRA military 4x4 originally developed by ACMAT (now part of Arquus). The ACMAT VLRA and its latest Arquus version are in service with military forces around the world. The new version has greater mobility, a larger payload capacity and increased protection. The VLRA vehicles have established a reputation for ruggedness, simplicity and autonomy, making them easy to maintain in remote or hostile environments. Parts are designed to be interchangeable, reducing the risk of breakdowns. While some vehicles of this type are developments of an original civilian chassis or vehicle, the VLRA-2 is military from the ground up.

Based on a heavy duty all-welded steel chassis, the VLRA-2 has beam-type axles with differential locks and parabolic multi-leaf springs. It is powered by

ARQUUS (ACMAT) VLRA-2
Country of origin: France
Manufacturer: Arquus (ACMAT)
Service: 2012–present
Operators: French Foreign Legion
Crew: 2, plus 12/19
Weight: 8000kg (17,636lbs)
Dimensions: Length 5.7m (18ft 8in), Width 2.2m (7ft 3in), Height 2.4m (7ft 9in)
Powerplant: Diesel engine
Range: 1400km (870 miles)
Speed: 110km/h (68mph)
Weapons: 12.7mm (0.5in) and 7.62mm (0.3in) machine guns, 40mm (1.6in) grenade launcher

HMMWV PATROL
US Army special forces in HMWWVs patrol south of Najaf after a heavy battle with Iraqi forces, March 2003.

LIGHT MEDIUM TACTICAL VEHICLE (LMTV)

Country of origin: United States

Manufacturer: BAE Systems

Service: 1996–present

Operators: US Special Forces

Crew: 4

Weight: 2.27 tonnes (2.5 tons)

Dimensions: Length 6.4m (20ft 10in), Width 2.43m (7ft 10in), Height 2.84m (9ft 3in)

Powerplant: Caterpillar 3115 ATAAC turbocharged diesel

Range: 645km (400 miles)

Speed: 44km/h (27mph)

Weapons: M2 .50 calibre machine gun; M240 7.62mm (0.3in) machine gun; Mk 19/ Mk 47 40mm (1.6in) grenade launcher; M249 SAW 5.56mm (0.21in) machine gun

a diesel engine with a six-speed ZF manual or five-speed automatic gearbox. The VLRA-2 is designed to be modular and can be adapted to multiple tasks. In troop-carrier mode, it can carry up to 14 military personnel in the back along with three in the cab. The vehicle can also be configured to carry 20 jerry cans of fuel or water for resupply. Other versions include multipurpose maintenance, command and control, or ambulance.

The VLRA-2 can be fitted with a 12.7mm (0.5in) machine gun on a ring mount and also a pedestal-mounted 7.62mm (0.3in) or 5.56mm (0.21in) machine gun. Smoke-grenade launchers can be fitted to the front of the vehicle. The vehicle has standard armour protection that can be supplemented if necessary with appliqué armour.

Other equipment includes a winch and a central tyre inflation system (CTIS). The VLRA-2 can be transported in fixed-wing aircraft like the C-130 Hercules or A400M, and also in the CH-47 Chinook helicopter.

Light Medium Tactical Vehicle (LMTV) 'War Pig'

The Light Medium Tactical Vehicle (LMTV), converted for special forces use, is a modification of the standard 2.27-tonne (2.5-ton) M1078 truck. Inspired by the Unimog used by the Special Air Service (SAS) as a support vehicle for Land Rover long-range patrols, especially in the first Gulf War, the LMTV provided similar support for US special forces Operational

Detachment Alpha units and their Ground Mobility Vehicles, such as HMMWVs. The large capacity for supplies in the LMTV allows special forces teams to survive for longer without replenishment, allowing the smaller vehicles to travel lighter and thus retain their mobility and overall effectiveness. Although primarily a supply vehicle, the LMTV is also able to carry an array of weaponry for either defence or attack. These include an M2 .50 calibre machine gun mounted at the rear and a pintle-mounted 7.62mm (0.3in) or 5.56mm (0.21in) machine gun adjacent to the commander's position. It can also mount a 40mm automatic grenade launcher. The LMTV can carry optional Javelin missiles or AT-4 rockets.

The M1078 truck was based on a design by Austrian manufacturer Steyr and was first fielded in 1996. The truck was manufactured by the Oshkosh Corporation after 2012. It is powered by a Caterpillar 3115 ATAAC turbo-diesel engine and has fully automatic transmission. It was replaced by the LMTV A2 in 2019.

HMT 600 (Coyote) 6x6

The HMT 600, known in the British Army as the Coyote, is the extended 6x6 version of the HMT 400, known in the British Army as the Jackal and in special forces circles as the Menacity.

The extra length and payload of the HMT 600 makes it useful as a mothership, carrying supplies for extended operations. This role was previously fulfilled for special forces by the Unimog. The HMT 600 can be fitted with a variety of mission-specific hampers as well as the necessary equipment to carry out operations. These include communications, ISTAR and force protection equipment. As a support vehicle, the emphasis may be on supplies but the HMT 600 can also be adapted to carry out force protection roles. It has a payload capacity in the rear of up to 3000kg (6614lb) and a flexible rear loading area.

HMT 600 COYOTE
Country of origin:
United Kingdom
Manufacturer: Supacat
Service: 2004–present
Operators: British Army
Crew: 4
Weight: 10,500kg (23,148lb)
Dimensions: Length 7.04m (23ft 1in), Width 2.05m (6ft 7in), Height 1.88m (6ft 2in)
Powerplant: Cummins 6.7 litre 6-cylinder diesel engine
Range: 700km (435 miles)
Speed: 120km/h (75mph)
Weapons: 12.7mm (0.5in) machine gun; 7.62mm (0.3in) machine gun; 40mm (1.6in) automatic grenade launcher

SAS Vehicles in Operation Trent

In November 2001, in the early days of Operation Enduring Freedom in Afghanistan, the UK's 22nd Special Air Service (SAS) carried out one of its largest post-World War II operations. Called Operation Trent, it involved an assault on an al-Qaeda-run facility at the base of the Koh-I-Malik mountain near the Pakistan border in Helmand Province. The facility was manned by up to 100 mostly al-Qaeda fighters.

A and G Squadrons SAS took part in the operation, which began with a high-altitude low opening (HALO) jump by SAS soldiers who secured the landing strip. Six C-130 Hercules aircraft of the US Air Force then arrived for a rapid landing, with the SAS vehicles racing off the back ramps as soon as the aircraft were on the ground. Thirty-six vehicles were deployed, including SAS 'Pinkie' Land Rovers, Kawasaki trail bikes and ACMAT VLRA liaison, reconnaissance and support vehicles.

Once the trail bikes had moved forward for rapid reconnaissance, followed by the other vehicles, dismounted SAS troopers assaulted the facility. They received covering fire from vehicle-mounted weapons, including 7.62mm (0.3in) GPMGs, 40mm (1.6in) grenade launchers and MILAN anti-tank missiles, as well as snipers who took up positions with L82A1 Barrett 0.5in anti-materiel rifles, spotting their targets with Leupold M series 10x magnification sights.

Essential supplies and ammunition, along with other back-up, were carried by the ACMAT VLRA vehicles. Rugged and dependable, they made an essential contribution to mission success.

SPECIAL FORCES RECON
A British special forces soldier inspects a deserted al-Qaida training camp on the outskirts of Kandahar airport, 2002.

There is an optional armour kit for protection against mine blasts, small-arms fire and shrapnel, but, due to its open architecture, the main protection for the HMT 600 is its speed, mobility and manoeuvrability. Mobility is enhanced by its variable, air-adjustable ride height suspension system. The vehicle is powered by a 6.7-litre six-cylinder Cummins diesel engine.

Armament includes a 12.7mm (0.5in) machine gun mounted on a ring as well as a 7.62mm (0.3in) medium machine gun or 40mm (1.6in) automatic grenade launcher. The vehicle is also fitted with smoke-grenade launchers to enable it to break contact when under enemy fire.

Optional extras for the HMT 600 include a remote weapons station, infrared (IR) lights, run-flat tyres and a self-recovery winch.

Jankel Light Tactical Transport Vehicle (LTTV)

Based on a Unimog U5000 civilian vehicle platform, the Jankel Light Tactical Transport Vehicle is a modular multi-role platform that can be adapted for various forms of military support. The armoured cab has been specially designed by Jankel to provide crew protection. Modular armour can be added to increase protection to both the cab and the rear cargo area. The windows are also armoured. The front window is divided into two sections and can be folded forward. The vehicle also features a roll-over protection system (ROPS) that can be folded when the vehicle is transported in aircraft such as the C-130 Hercules or A400M.

The LTTV can be fitted with an electric self-recovery winch, an electric loading winch, black-out lights, infrared (IR) lights and run-flat tyre technology. A cold-weather pack is also available.

The LTTV is fitted with a weapon ring that can mount a .50mm or 7.62mm (0.3in) machine gun. A front swing-arm can mount either a 7.62mm (0.3in) or 5.56mm (0.21in) machine gun. A swing-arm machine gun mount is also located in the rear of the vehicle.

The rear compartment can carry eight fully equipped and armed troops, in addition to the driver and commander in the cab.

The LTTV is powered by a Mercedes-Benz 4.8 litre, four-cylinder, four-stroke diesel engine. It has a semi-automatic Mercedes-Benz gearbox with eight forward and six reverse gears.

The Belgian Ministry of Defence has ordered 199 LTTVs for its special forces and para-commandos, in addition to the Fox RDV also supplied by Jankel Armouring.

Supacat Light Reconnaissance Vehicle (LRV) 600

The LRV 600 is the extended version of the LRV 400, enabling the vehicle to carry 50 per cent more payload and significantly increasing capacity for supplies. One of the unique features of the vehicle is

SUPACAT LRV 600
Country of origin:
United Kingdom
Manufacturer: Supacat
Service: 2012–present
Operators: N/A
Crew: 4
Weight: 5500kg (12,125lb)
Dimensions: Length 3.63m (11ft 9in), Width 1.83m (6ft), Height 1.80m (5ft 9in)
Powerplant: V6 3 litre diesel
Range: N/A
Speed: 160km/h (99mph)
Weapons: 12.7mm (0.5in) machine gun; 7.62mm (0.3in) GPMG

that it can be extended from the base 4x4 version if required and the manufacturer claims that it is the only vehicle in the world that can be converted in this way. The primary role of the LRV 600 is to act as a support vehicle for special forces patrols with more compact vehicles.

The basis of the vehicle is the chassis and the automotive system of the Land Rover Discovery, which have been adapted by Supacat for specialist military purposes. It is fitted with a Supacat double wishbone air suspension at both the front and rear and this can be adjusted for height. Along with the bump stops, this allows the vehicle to be lowered in order to provide a stable firing platform.

The vehicle is powered by a V6 3-litre turbo-diesel engine linked to an eight-speed automatic transmission. It has both high and low permanent four-wheel drive with a centre differential lock.

The combination of Land Rover and Supacat engineering enables the vehicle to travel at high speeds through challenging terrain and it can be used for a wide variety of special forces missions, including reconnaissance, strike missions and border patrol.

Helicopter insertion

Despite the fact that is it larger than the 4x4 LRV variant, the LRV 600 can still be carried in the hold of a CH-47 Chinook helicopter, making it a viable and practical vehicle for fast insertion during special forces missions.

The LRV 600 can carry a 12.7mm (0.5in) heavy machine gun mounted on a ring at the rear of the vehicle. There is a mount for a 7.62mm (0.3in) general purpose machine gun next to the passenger seat at the front of the vehicle. The vehicle is fitted with smoke-grenade launchers at both the front and the rear.

Optional extras include run-flat tyres, infrared (IR) lights, forward- and rear-facing IR cameras and a self-recovery winch.

Dutch Military Vehicles Anaconda

Based on the Iveco Daily light armoured chassis, the DMV Anaconda is a compact troop carrier and patrol vehicle designed to fulfil the requirements of the Royal Netherlands Marine Corps in remote areas. The rugged chassis and its 4x4 capabilities enable the vehicle to perform support and patrol missions in rough terrain.

The standard configuration allows for four crew, including the driver and commander, but the vehicle can be adapted if necessary to carry up to nine personnel. The open-door layout allows for ease of movement and rapid engagement if necessary. The open roof structure includes a ring mount for a 12.7mm (0.5in) or 7.62mm (0.3in) machine gun. The Anaconda is powered by a 3-litre diesel engine with an eight-speed fully automatic drive train.

DUTCH MILITARY VEHICLES ANACONDA
Country of origin: The Netherlands
Manufacturer: Defense Materiel Organisation (DMO)/Deba Trucks
Service: 2018–present
Operators: Korps Mariniers (Royal Dutch Marine Corps)
Crew: 4
Weight: 3900kg (8598lb)
Dimensions: Length 5.27m (17ft 3in), Width 2.26m (7ft 4in), Height 2.27m (7ft 4in)
Powerplant: 3 litre Iveco diesel engine
Range: 1000km (621 miles)
Speed: 110km/h (68mph)
Weapons: 12.7mm (0.5in) machine gun; 2 x 7.62mm (0.3in) machine gun

DMV ANACONDA INTERIOR
The interior of the Anaconda military vehicle showing the readily available 7.62mm (0.3in) machine gun for forward and side defence.

NON-STANDARD TACTICAL & COMMERCIAL VEHICLES

The word 'technical' as applied to customized civilian 4x4s is thought to have its roots in the civil war in Somalia in the 1990s to describe the vehicles used by armed supporters who would otherwise have been banned by regulations. The so called 'technical advisers' brought with them an archetypal vehicle that would also assume the name 'technical'. This vehicle was usually a 4x4 pick-up, with or without an extended cab, with a flatbed at the back on which was mounted a weapon, usually in the form of a heavy machine gun. The main characteristic of these vehicles was their simplicity. They were off-the-shelf commercial vehicles with the minimum modifications required for their role.

TOYOTA PICK-UP

An American special forces soldier mans a machine gun as he rides on the back of a pick-up truck en route to Gardez, Afghanistan, 2002.

The NSCV provides … a low visibility vehicle capability to conduct operations in politically or operationally constrained permissive, semi-permissive or denied areas.
– US Colonel John Reim explained their purpose in 2018

SOMALIA, 1991

A technical vehicle typical of those used by factions in the civil wars in Somalia in 1991. Commercial 4x4 pick-ups such as this one wielded considerable firepower and were also regarded as a status symbol by local warlords.

The roots of such vehicles go back a long way to the adapted Model T Ford cars mounted with Vickers .50 calibre machine guns that were used by British forces against allies of the Turkish occupying army in the Middle East. These in turn inspired the development of the Long Range Desert Group (LRDG) in World War II, where Chevrolet and Ford 30cwt trucks were armed with a variety of weapons for long-range reconnaissance and offensive operations against Axis forces in North Africa. However, technicals in the modern sense are associated with those vehicles used by the Polisario guerrillas in the 1970s during their war against Moroccan forces, and the conflict between Chad and Libya in the 1980s. Japanese-made technicals were so prevalent in this conflict that *Time* magazine dubbed it 'The Great Toyota War'. The speed and mobility of the technicals used by the Chadian forces with weapons supplied by France gave them an advantage over the slower-moving military vehicles used by their opponents.

During the war in Afghanistan from 2001 (Operation Enduring Freedom), technicals were used by the Taliban as well as its NATO-backed opponents, the Northern Alliance. From 2003, during the invasion of Iraq by coalition forces, Fedayeen (Islamic military groups) loyal to Saddam Hussein used technicals to scour the desert searching for US and allied special forces. A British Special Boat Service (SBS) patrol was compromised by these roving technicals, while an Australian Special Air Service Regiment (SASR) had to fight them off. Tehnicals would continue to be used in other conflicts, such as those in Libya, Syria and Yemen.

Some of the vehicles most widely used as technicals are the Toyota Hilux, the Land Cruiser and the Tacoma, as well as an assortment of other 4x4 pick-ups including Ford Rangers and Land Rover Defenders. Special forces did not take long to appreciate the value of such vehicles, especially for operations where they wanted to maintain a low profile.

WAR ON TERROR
US Army special forces soldiers drive through the streets of Kandahar, Afghanistan, on the way to their security post at the new interim prime minister Hamid Karzai's compound, December 2001.

Non-Standard Commercial Vehicles (NSCVs) and Non-Standard Tactical Vehicles (NSTVs)

NSCV or NSTV are the terms for a technical-style vehicle modified specifically for special forces. Different special forces units had their own shopping list of adaptations which were made either in-theatre with the vehicles that they had obtained or customized in the United States or elsewhere. US Special Operations Command (USSOCOM) purchased

AFGHANISTAN OPERATIONS
US special forces troops climb out of a truck at Bamiyan airport in Bamiyan, Afghanistan, 2002.

several Toyota Tacomas during the war in Afghanistan that were then modified to include mounts for M240 or M249 machine guns, antennae for satellite and UHF/VHF communications, Blue Force Trackers, infrared (IR) lights and winches. Standard vehicle lighting systems were either rewired or disconnected. The USSOCOM list of vehicles continued to expand to include the Toyota Hilux double cab and Land Cruiser 200. Adaptations included a reinforced chassis and upgraded suspension to cope with the extra weight of weaponry, ammunition and optional ballistic armour, roof racks, IR lights, C4ISR and navigation systems and run-flat tyres. UK special forces also used NSTVs, including the Land Rover Defender and the Toyota Hilux.

As demand grew, specialist contractors would strip down imported commercial vehicles such as the Toyota Hilux or Land Cruiser 200 and convert them to the standard required by the special forces. Challenges were sometimes encountered, such as working around on-board computers that did not recognize the adaptations. Bolt-on armour was found to be preferable to welded armour as the welding seams could be vulnerable to ballistic penetration. Some parts of the original vehicles were removed and discarded, some removed, modified and reinstalled, and some removed to be reinstalled later. Other modifications included the engine cooling system which needed to be adapted to cope with the extra demands placed on the vehicle, including extra weight from armaments and ballistic armour, as well as mobility in challenging terrain in extreme heat.

The phenomenon of the civilian technical vehicle and the special forces Non-Standard Tactical Vehicle led to the development of more specifically militarized vehicles, such as the Jankel Fox RRV-x featured earlier, or the Arquus Trapper. Navistar Defense and Indigen Armor went a step further with their International Special Operations Tactical Vehicle (SOTV). Instead of upgrading an existing commercial vehicle, they built a ground-up military vehicle that could then be 'skinned' to look like the ubiquitous Toyota Hilux. The advantage of this approach was that the mission-ready military platform did not have to be adapted to do things that it was not designed for and the users did not have to sacrifice room, for example, where ballistic armour add-ons intruded into the available vehicle space. The SOTV was designed to be 10 per cent larger than the vehicles it mimicked in order to give users maximum space while being compact enough to fit into the hold a CH-47 Chinook helicopter.

While demand from special forces continues there is some debate about the viability of Non-Standard Tactical Vehicles among the special forces community.

BRITISH ARMY LAND ROVER
A British Army WMIK Land Rover manned by paratroopers near Camp Bastion, Afghanistan. With its multiple 7.62mm (0.3in) machine guns, this military vehicle has many similarities to a technical.

Purpose-Built Non-Standard Commercial Vehicle (PB-NSCV)

Fielding a wide array of Non-Standard Tactical Vehicles (NSTVs) or Non-Standard Commercial Vehicles (NSCVs) presents the largest user of such vehicles, namely US Special Operations Command (USSOCOM), with a

considerable challenge in not only upgrading the various types of commercial vehicle to the required standard but also providing a myriad of spare parts, many of which are not interchangeable either between models of the same manufacturer let alone between models made by different manufacturers, such as Ford or Toyota. Having examined its support commitments for about 500 of the vehicles that it fields, US Special Operations Command has explored an alternative route. The idea is to build a ground-up military vehicle with inherent strength and mobility for all mission requirements, including protection, armaments and electronic communications, not to mention payload capacity. In order to maintain the low profile of a Non-Standard Tactical or Commercial Vehicle, the new vehicle would then be 'skinned' to mimic the appearance of regularly used commercial vehicles such as the Ford Ranger or Toyota Land Cruiser.

The requirement laid down by USSOCOM would be for the skinned vehicle to pass unnoticed at a range of 90m (330ft) and at a speed of 55km/h (35mph). These specific requirements speak very much of the drawing board and not of the realities of deployment. Another challenge and requirement would be the audible signature. The skinned vehicle would also need to sound like the vehicle it attempts to replicate.

Special forces requirments

USSOCOM's shopping list of requirements continues. The new vehicle would have better overall performance than its civilian-based counterparts and thus would be able to carry out more demanding tasks. These performance levels would not be affected by the heavy payloads demanded by the various special forces mission sets that the vehicle is likely to encounter. Despite this capability, the vehicle's own weight would be limited to 4309kg (9500lb) and its size and weight would enable it to be transported in the hold of an MH-47 Chinook helicopter flown by the 160th Special Operations Aviation Regiment (SOAR) or a CH-53E Super Stallion or CH-53K King Stallion helicopter flown by the US Marine Corps. It should also be transportable by C-130 Hercules and similar fixed-wing aircraft. The vehicle must also have sufficient modularity so that different special forces units can adapt it to their mission requirements.

Special forces vehicles also need to carry a sophisticated array of electronic equipment in order to carry out their roles. This may include encrypted military communications systems, signals intelligence equipment to track enemy movements by their phone and radio signals, radio-direction finding and also IED jamming devices.

Armament for such a vehicle would typically include a .50 calibre M2 machine gun with the possibility of a weapon being mounted in a remote-controlled weapon station (RCWS). In 'technical' style, a pick-up version would mount a 7.62mm (0.3in) or 5.56mm (0.21in) machine gun in the rear. While the concept of a purpose-built NSCV seems to make sense from the

ARQUUS TRAPPER VT14
The Arquus Trapper VT14 delivered to the French armed forces is based on a Ford Everest chassis, demonstrating how a commercial vehicle can be the basis of an advanced mission-specific military vehicle.

perspective of mission efficiency, rationalization of assets and cost-benefit analysis, it raises as many questions and issues as it seems to resolve. The various types of vehicle that SOF currently use are available and familiar in some regions but not in others. Therefore, any chameleon-like military vehicle would need to have its camouflage 'skins' available to match locally available vehicles if it is not to stick out like a sore thumb and compromise its occupants. The PB-NSCC might successfully mimic the overall look of a particular model of commercial vehicle from a distance but closer examination is likely to reveal tell-tale signs of its role. The most obvious give-aways are antennae and, of course, weapons. This raises the question of to what extent special forces can expect to hide in plain sight, whether in adapted commercial vehicles or purpose-built military ones.

Perhaps the most that can be expected of a Non-Standard Tactical or Commercial Vehicle or a Purpose Built Non-Standard Commercial Vehicle is that it can soften the lines of a special forces presence to make it less overt and to provide sufficient protection if the SOF becomes involved in a fire-fight that it would otherwise seek to avoid.

SECURITY DETAIL

US Army special forces soldiers drive through the streets of Kandahar, Afghanistan, in Toyota Hiluxes, 2001.

Toyota Hilux

The Toyota Hilux was first announced in 1968 and has now reached its eighth generation, along with numerous facelifts. Having begun as a compact pick-up, it evolved into a mid-size pick-up. Over 18 million Hilux vehicles have been produced since it was first launched and it can be found in various

forms all around the world, including Australia, the Middle East, Africa and South America.

During its more than half-century of life, the Hilux has won a reputation for ruggedness and reliability that has made it legendary. For this reason, it has also been favoured by militants and insurgents, who have used it as a base for mounting weapons, including heavy machine guns, making it the king of the technicals.

The secret of the Hilux's famed indestructibility is its simplicity. Fewer parts means that there is less chance of things going wrong. The original box frame that was used to build the vehicle chassis was also stronger than the more common C-frame and also meant that it could be lighter, as a stronger construction required less metal. However, the weakness of the box-frame design was its susceptibility to rust, so Toyota moved to a mixed box and C-frame design on later vehicles. The 4-litre engine resulted from long periods of development on various Toyota models and the engine block was a mixture of iron and nickel, which gave it greater strength. It was also designed with a long-stroke piston design, which provided greater torque.

In 2014, it was reported that the British Special Air Service (SAS) would be taking delivery of about 60 Toyota Hilux 4x4 vehicles. Although by then the British Government was planning a draw down of British forces in Afghanistan, the vehicles would be well suited to low-profile counter-insurgency operations in other conflicts where the familiar Hilux

TOYOTA HILUX
With its extraordinarily rugged chassis, the Toyota Hilux is one of the most popular choices for special forces when seeking a low-profile commercial type of vehicle.

TOYOTA LAND CRUISER
Technicals, such as this converted Toyota Land Cruiser carrying an anti-aircraft gun, proved to be extremely effective, even when faced with armoured military vehicles.

was unlikely to draw too much unwelcome attention. Commonly available in parts of the world were its rugged durability and ease of maintenance are genuinely valued, the Hilux provided special forces with an easy-to-maintain low-cost solution.

Upgrades to the Hilux for special forces use included rewired lighting systems and the addition of infrared lights, fittings for advanced communications systems, military specification stowage racks for fuel, water and other supplies, and mounts for heavy or medium machine guns.

Toyota Land Cruiser (76, 78, 79 and 200 series)

Apart from the Toyota Hilux, the Toyota Land Cruiser 200, first launched in 2007, was one of the vehicles most favoured by US Special Operations Command (USSOCOM) for upgrade to the status of a special forces' Non-Standard Tactical Vehicle (NSTV). Other versions of the Land Cruiser have also been employed both as technicals and as NSTVs.

The Toyota Land Cruiser is the company's longest-running model, having been first launched in 1951, since when over 10 million cars have been sold worldwide. It has been produced in a variety of versions, including a convertible, station wagon, hard top and as cab designs, including single and double cab.

The original inspiration for the Land Cruiser was the Willys Jeep, which Japanese forces captured in the Philippines and sought to emulate. During the Korean War the United States asked Toyota to build another Jeep-based vehicle to resupply their hard-pressed forces. The Toyota version, known as the Jeep BJ, was larger than the standard Jeep and the name had to be changed due to protests from Willys about using the Jeep designation. Inspired by the British Land Rover, Toyota chose to call their vehicle the Land Cruiser. The Land Cruiser went from strength to strength. Benefiting from high Japanese production values, it built a reputation for durability and dependability only matched by its sister vehicle, the Hilux.

Land Cruiser 70 series

The LC70 series has been produced since 1984, replacing the legendary 40 series as the definitive, rugged, off-road workhorse. The 70 series includes a variety of models, those from 70 to 74 referring to two-door short- and medium-based models, and model numbers 75, 78 and 79 referring to long wheel-base versions that were produced in either two-door or pick-up models.

Land Cruiser 76

The LC76 is a five-door, five-seater car that is designed to be a straightforward, practical, no-frills 4x4. It has plenty of internal room and an uncomplicated interior, making it useful and adaptable.

The LC76 is powered by a 4.5 litre turbo-diesel V8 engine with a low-range transfer case.

ARMOURED TOYOTA LAND CRUISER
Members of the German elite Spezialeinsatzkommando (SEK) police tactical unit stand in front of their specialized armoured V8 Toyota Land Cruiser vehicles. Adapted commercial 4x4s are often a first choice for specialist police and special forces units.

Land Cruiser 78

The LC78 series has become a standard vehicle for many front-line organizations that require the highest standards of dependability and mobility. Operators of the LC78 include UN agencies and Non-Governmental Organizations (NGOs) which benefit from its large seating capacity allied to its first-class off-road abilities in often hard-to-reach areas.

The LC78 is powered by a six cylinder diesel engine linked to a five speed manual transmission. The rugged chassis of the LC78 has made it a suitable vehicle for up-armouring by contractors who supply protected vehicles to civilian and military clients.

Land Cruiser 200

The LC200 is regarded by many as having an optimum balance between rugged strength and comfort. Launched in the 2008, it has received two facelifts since then and has now been replaced by the LC300.

The LC200 was produced in a variety of trims, the base version being the GX that was aimed at businesses and specialist organizations, including police and forestry teams. Its powerful V8 engine and sturdy chassis enabled it to carry considerable weight without compromising performance or mobility.

USSOCOM Order Armoured Land Cruiser 200s

The US research and development organization Batelle received an order in 2020 to armour and upgrade 229 Land Cruiser 200 vehicles for USSOCOM. The vehicles were due for delivery and deployment in 2022 through to 2023 and would incorporate the complex systems demanded by special forces. The order was also an indication of USSOCOM's continued interest in vehicles that enabled special forces to maintain a low profile in areas where an overt military presence would attract unwelcome attention.

Toyota Tacoma

First produced in January 1995, the Toyota Tacoma is a 4x4 pick-up similar in size to the Toyota Hilux but adapted to the requirements of the US and South American markets. It was perceived that these markets wanted a more comfortable vehicle with better handling characteristics than the more utilitarian Hilux.

Ford Ranger

Ford's answer to the Toyota Hilux, the Ford Ranger has existed in various forms since the 1980s. The standard international version relevant to special forces use was produced from May 2011, largely based on the version produced in Australia. The T6 model was not sold in the United States between 2011 and 2018, and special forces conversions were carried out on the international version. The Ford Ranger pick-ups used by USSOCOM were upgraded by Battelle, a company with similar technology solutions

TACOMA PICK-UP
US special forces near Gardez, Afghanistan. Although this Toyota Tacoma pick-up looks relatively normal from the outside, it hosts a range of adaptations, including an M240 machine gun (pictured), armour and communications equipment.

to the UK-based Ricardo. Battelle was involved in Toyota pick-ups, such as the Hilux and Land Cruiser, and extended the list to include the Ford Ranger. Upgrades include armour plating, armoured glass and run-flat tyres. The suspension is also strengthened to carry the extra weight.

Ford Ranger Military Concept Vehicle

The Ford Ranger's ruggedness and suitability for militarization was recognized by the UK-based development company Ricardo, which has a long history of developing engines for British Army tanks going back to World War I, as well as the more recent Ocelot/Foxhound light protected vehicle. Ricardo developed a concept vehicle based on the Ford Ranger, drawing on its versatility, durability and towing capacity. The vehicle could be fitted with a variety of engines including Ford's own 2-litre EcoBlue turbo-diesel powertrain linked to an advanced all-speed automatic transmission.

The Ricardo Ranger concept included armoured ballistic floor protection and armoured glass, skid plates to protect the radiator, fuel tank and powertrain, light but heavy-duty front and rear bumpers, an upgraded electrical system to allow for electromagnetic compatibility protection, a ring-mount weapons system, and upgraded suspension, brakes and wheels to cope with increased weight and towing capacity. The vehicle is also compatible with C4I (command, control, communications, computers and intelligence) systems. Some of these developments resulted from cooperation with Polaris Government and Defense in the United States.

Ford adapted its controls and displays so that they could be more easily visible for military personnel wearing night vision goggles.

FORD RANGER ON PATROL
Aghan National Army soldiers return to their base in Farah province in a Ford Ranger 4x4 pick-up. Such vehicles could be adapted relatively quickly for military service.

Ford Ranger XLT for the Polish Army

The Ford Ranger XLT, adapted for military use by Glomex Ms Polska, was selected by the Polish Ministry of Defence as its light-duty all-terrain pick-up. The vehicle was upgraded to include metal underbody protection, aluminium hard-top roofing and run-flat tyres. The vehicle is powered by Ford's 2.0 litre EcoBlue TDCi engine linked to a six-speed manual gearbox with either 2x2 or 4x4 transmission.

Navistar Defense Special Operations Tactical Vehicle (SOTV)

The Special Operations Tactical Vehicle was a new approach to the challenge of modifying commercial vehicles by producing a purpose-built military platform and adapting it to replicate a commonly available commercial vehicle.

The vehicle was designed by Navistar Defense in conjunction with Indigen Armour for use by United States Special Operations Command (USSOCOM). The vehicle has a ground-up military grade platform that can carry a payload of almost 1360kg (3000lb) and can manage both the weight of its own armour package as well as all the equipment that special forces soldiers would expect to carry. This means also that it retains all of its mobility and manoeuvrability in demanding terrain and has a higher operational capability than an adapted commercial vehicle.

FORD RANGER XLT

Ford Ranger XLT vehicles are ceremonially handed over to the Polish Army. The vehicles were upgraded to military standard by a Polish company to meet the demanding requirements of a modern military force.

119

How to Convert a Standard Commercial 4x4 into a Special Forces 4x4

The transformation of a standard commercial vehicle into an identical special forces one may not be noticeable on the surface but involves the addition of about 1814kg (3000lb) of armour and military specification equipment.

1. A plan is made at design stage to work out how all the different military specification fittings and adaptations will interact with the original vehicle specification, including electrical components, shocks and springs as well as armour and tactical additions.

2. The original vehicle is stripped down to its bare frame, with each part labelled ready for re-installation later in the process.
3. Where relevant, OEM parts are replaced by specially sourced parts designed to cope with the extra demands that will be placed on the vehicle.

4. The metal structure of the vehicle is reinforced to cope with demanding military standards.

5. Electrical and mechanical substructures are built which will be installed in the final build phase.

6. About 907kg (2000lb) of armour is added to the vehicle in such a way as to reduce weaknesses caused by welding.

Armoured doors are fitted, including windows with state-of-the-art armoured glass.

7. Tough metal bumpers are fitted to the front of the vehicle to be concealed under the original vehicle front.

8. The vehicle is reassembled so that it is almost impossible to tell the difference from what it looked like at the beginning of the process.

9. The vehicle receives quality checks and is driven over a tough 4x4 testing ground.

The SOTV can be fitted with a collapsible turret and main weapon station while secondary weapons' mounts can be fitted with a variety of medium or light machine guns. Built around a monocoque welded safety cell, the armour package is designed to protect against ballistic threats and shrapnel to B6 standard. Bullet-proof glass also protects the crew from a variety of threats, including small-arms fire.

The SOTV is powered by a Cummins diesel engine linked to an Allison transmission. The vehicle has four-wheel independent suspension. The front suspension consists of double-wishbone arms and coil-over shocks. The rear suspension has semi-trailing arms with coil-over shocks. The suspension system includes hydraulic bump stops, front and rear.

The SOTV can be transported in the hold of a CH-47 or MH-47 Chinook helicopter.

Nissan Navara

The Nissan Navara compact 4x4 pick-up was first produced in 1997 and has received numerous upgrades and facelifts over the years, the last being in 2020. It is also sold under different names in different markets, and is known as the Frontier in the United States. The Nissan Navara has been assembled in its various forms around the world, including the United States, Mexico, Brazil, Spain, Thailand and Malaysia.

The Nissan Navara was one of the 4x4 pick-ups selected for upgrading for special forces use and was also used by the Italian special forces Navy Operational Raiders Group (or GOI, Gruppo Operativo Incursori) in deployment in Afghanistan.

NISSAN NAVARA
The Nissan Navarra was another of the highly rated 4x4 pick-ups selected by special forces for specialized upgrading. Reinforcements to the metal structure and suspension systems to support armour protection and other systems would be invisible to the eye.

MOTORCYCLES & QUAD BIKES

The military motorcycle has a long history and is intimately tied up with the development of the motorcycle. In England, the Birmingham Small Arms (BSA) factory, which was involved in making armaments such as Lee-Enfield rifles and Lewis machine guns, was also a bicycle maker that in 1905 extended its product line into motorcycles. Other bicycle manufacturers, including Ariel, Matchless, Velocette and Triumph, did the same. These manufacturers supplied British forces with motorcycles in World War I, where Triumph earned the accolade 'The Trusty Triumph'. Healthy competition led to new developments, including the ground-breaking 1938 500 Speed Twin by Ariel, which was light, compact, easy-revving and powerful.

CHRISTINI AWD TRAIL MOTORCYCLE
Airmen from Special Tractics Training Squadron, 24th Special Operations Wing, ride Christini AWD trail motorcycles in a vehicle column that also includes Polaris MRZR D2 light all-terrain vehicles.

123

Motorcycles in World War I were highly prized as a means of sending messages at a time when battlefield telephone communications were rather basic. Despatch riders whizzed around on hazardous roads, dodging sniper fire to deliver vital orders.

When World War II broke out, most of the British motorcycle manufacturers were given contracts to supply military specification motorcycles. BSA would produce 130,000 of its M20 model alongside its armaments production. Triumph was also heavily involved in production, despite losing its Coventry factory to German bombs. Norton produced its 16H and Big 4 motorcycles, while Royal Enfield produced the WD/RE 'Flying Flea', a mini-motorcycle small enough to be carried by airborne forces. In the United States, Harley-Davidson produced its classic WL model, which would also have a profound influence in the post-war era on biker culture. Although some British models, such as the Norton Big 4, were also produced with a sidecar, the real experts in this area proved to be the Germans. The *Blitzkrieg* that took Europe by storm relied upon speed and the spearhead was often fast-moving motorcycle and sidecar units. These Kradschutzen units, organized within panzer formations, carried out rapid mobile assault and reconnaissance. German industry produced a wide variety of motorcycles for the Wehrmacht, including the BMW R75 and sidecar, the

HARLEY DAVIDSON WLA
The Harley Davidson WLA was one of the most widely used motorcycles by US and Allied forces during World War II. Motorcycles such as these were mostly used by despatch riders or for escort duties.

DKW RT125 and NZ250, a variety of models by NSU, and the Zundapp 600cc KSW sidecar rigs, including the KS 750 flat twin. Other countries produced their own motorcycles, including Belgium with its FN M12 military model, and France with its Gnome-Rhône 750 Armee.

While the *Blitzkrieg* in Western Europe mostly happened during hot summer weather when the ground was dry, the invasion of Soviet Russia in Operation Barbarossa soon ran into the Russian winter and the snow melt. Vehicles of all types were bogged down and the heavy motorcycles, with their low ground clearance, fared badly. Their low-slung air filter filled with mud, which also got into the motors. In many ways, the era of the big military motorcycle was over.

Something else had happened that pushed the military motorcycle into the sidelines – the Wilys Jeep. Here was a four-wheel drive light vehicle with plenty of power that could go almost everywhere and was both rugged and stable.

Leaping forward to the first Gulf War in 1991, the motorcycles that made brief appearances were somewhat different to their World War II predecessors. These were high-riding trail bikes bred to tackle rough terrain. Nimble and speedy, they presented a low profile and were seen ahead of special forces columns, probing the Iraqi desert ready to swiftly report back on any signs of trouble.

TRAINING EXERCISE
A US Army soldier with 1st Battalion, 1st Special Forces Group (Airborne) prepares to ride a Kawasaki KLR 650 on to a CH-53E Super Stallion of 1st Marine Aircraft Wing on Okinawa, Japan.

HARLEY-DAVIDSON MT350
A Royal Marine Commando of 3 Brigade on a Harley Davidson MT350. Originally built in the UK as the Armstrong MT500, this motorcycle became standard issue for both UK and other NATO forces.

Speed, agility, mobility and a low profile were the aspects of the new model military motorcycle that would appeal to special forces. As ever, there was a thirst for new technology. The Christini AWD motorbike seemed to be made for special forces. Here was a bike that could go almost anywhere along the most unpredictable routes, allowing special forces to move quickly into position to carry out observations or call in air strikes. Special forces were put through specialized training in how to use motorcycles to their advantage. Quickly gaining high ground and keeping the enemy guessing where you are going and where you have come from are some of the advantages of fast trail bikes. With the development of silent electric power, special forces will also have the advantage of a silent approach.

Armstrong MT500 and Harley-Davidson MT350

First supplied to the British Army in 1984, the Armstrong MT500 motorcycles were produced by the Armstrong company until 1987, when production was taken over by Harley-Davidson in the United States. The Harley version, called the MT350, would remain in service until 2000. The MT500 was also a standard motorcycle for other NATO countries.

Fitted with a Rotax motor, the Armstrong and Harley-Davidson motorcycles were designed to be soldier-proof and were fitted with detachable pannier boxes at the front as well as a rifle scabbard on the back right-hand side. The motorcycle was designed to cope well with both paved roads and off-road conditions. Armstrong MT500 motorcycles were used in the first Gulf War in 1991 by British Special Air Service (SAS) outriders ahead of the SAS column of Land Rovers and Unimogs that entered the Iraqi desert from Saudi Arabia on the search and destroy mission against Iraqi Scud ballistic missiles. With their relatively low profile and high speed, the motorcycles could provide advance warning of any enemy contact.

ARMSTRONG MT500

Country of origin:
United Kingdom
Manufacturer: Armstrong-CCM
Service: 1984–present
Operators: British Army
Crew: 1
Weight: 160kg (352lbs)
Powerplant: Rotax 481.3cc air-cooled single cylinder 4-stroke, 4-valve
Range: 193km (120 miles)
Speed: 152km/h (95mph)

ARMSTRONG MT500

A British Army despatch rider on an Armstrong MT500 motorcycle during the first Gulf War in 1991. The tan camouflage for the bike is more appropriate for the environment than the temperate camouflage uniform worn by the soldier.

KAWASAKI KLR-250

Country of origin: Japan
Manufacturer: Kawasaki
Service: 1984–present
Operators: US special forces;
US Marine Corps; US Air Force
Special Operations Command
Crew: 1
Weight: 118kg (260lbs)
Powerplant: Kawasaki 249cc
4-stroke single cylinder
Range: 340km (210 miles)
Speed: N/A

Kawasaki KLR-250

The Kawasaki KLR-250 is a multi-purpose trail and road bike produced between 1984 and 2005. It was used by the United States military, including US Special Operations, the US Marine Corps and the US Air Force. The motorcycles were used for carrying messages between military units as well as reconnaissance.

Kawasaki KLR-650

The Kawasaki KLR-650 replaced the KLR-250 in US military use and was given different military designations according to the military branch in which it was used.

M1030: this is a ruggedized military version of the original KLR-650. It was used for carrying forward observers to their positions, as well as reconnaissance. It was designed to cope equally well with road and trail conditions, making it highly adaptable for military operations.

M1030M1: this model of the motorcycle has been developed as a diesel version for the US Marine Corps.

M1030M1E: this version was designed for the United Kingdom military and for other European NATO nations.

Kawasaki KLX-110

The Kawasaki KLX-110 is a small bike and has been used in military operations where its compact size is particularly useful.

US Air Force Special Operations Command (AFSOC) Special Forces Combat Rescue Officers use the KLX-110 for rapid battlefield engagement, as well as airfield surveys. The motorbike can be easily stowed in the hold of a helicopter for fast insertion or carried by a range of military vehicles, including the Ground Mobility Vehicle (GMV).

Suzuki DS80

This mini-bike is used by the US Rangers as an easily portable fast means of transport that can be quickly off-loaded from a helicopter to provide rapid reconnaissance.

Kawasaki KLX110 mini-bike

The Kawasaki KLX110 mini-bike is used by US Air Force Special Forces Command (AFSOC) Combat Controllers who need to carry out rapid airfield reconnaissance prior to parachute or aircraft landing operations.

Christini AWD Motorcycle

The Christini AWD Military Edition motorcycle is based on the Christini AWD 450E and 450-DS models. The motorcycle incorporates a unique

KAWASAKI KLR-650
Country of origin: Japan
Manufacturer: Kawasaki
Service: 2004–present
Operators: US Marine Corps; US special forces; UK armed forces; NATO armed forces
Crew: 1
Weight: 177kg (390lbs)
Powerplant: 584cc diesel engine
Range: 640km (400 miles)
Speed: 136km/h (85mph)

KAWASAKI KLR-650
A US Marine prepares to board a CH-53 Sea Stallion on board USS *Tarawa* riding an M103M1 diesel motorcycle based on the Kawasaki KLR-650.

CHRISTINI AWD

Country of origin: United States
Manufacturer: Christini
Service: 2016–present
Operators: US Navy SEALs;
US Air Force Special Tactics;
UK military
Crew: 1
Weight: 126kg (278lbs)
Powerplant: 450cc 4-stroke
Range: N/A
Speed: N/A

CHRISTINI AWD

US special forces prepare to deploy in front of a UH-60 Black Hawk helicopter. The all-wheel-drive system on the Christinia AWD provides exceptional mobility for special forces over challenging terrain.

system whereby a series of shafts and gears power the front wheel. The system is enclosed within the frame and fork tubes. It is a power-efficient system, losing only one per cent of power and adding only 6.8kg (15lbs) of weight. The Christini AWD motorcycle has been evaluated by several special forces units and is in service with the US Navy SEALs and US Air Force Special Forces Command. It has also been evaluated abroad, including Jordan, the United Arab Emirates and the United Kingdom.

The testing and evaluations carried out by the Army Special Operations Research Element in January 2010 concluded that the 'increase in traction stabilizes the bike, reducing the fatigue on the operator, while negotiating rough terrain'. It also enabled the bike to operate in areas that would be inaccessible to a standard motorcycle, such as deep sand. The US Air Force assessors came to similar conclusions.

To bring the motorcycle up to military standard, a number of alterations were made, including modification of the saddle for longer journeys, the addition of heavy duty suspension to carry heavy combat loads, an enlarged bullet-resistant radiator, run-flat tyres, a headlight system that can be switched from white light to infrared (IR) at the press of a button, and an anti-stall clutch, enabling the bike to brake to a halt without the engine stalling. The Christini AWD is used for scouting, reconnaissance and communications, as well as getting special forces operators quickly into positions where they can carry out tasks while maintaining a low profile.

Quad bikes

While the standard military motorcycle has largely fallen off the shopping list of many military procurement agencies, except for bespoke special forces versions, a new kid has appeared on the block. This has handlebars and a saddle, like a standard motorcycle, but it also has four chunky wheels. Farmers have been on the case for years, using quads for everything from shepherding sheep to carrying fence posts up muddy hills. Now the military have caught up and the more they use them the more they seem to like them.

Honda first introduced a three-wheel ATV in 1969, which proved popular with farmers and hunters in the United States. Another version came out in the 1980s but by then there were problems with the three-wheel set up, which can be unstable. Trail bike manufacturers such as Yamaha and Suzuki came up with four-wheel versions and these soon caught on. Polaris was not far behind. The United States military began to adopt them and the British Army started operating them in Helmand province, Afghanistan. Soldiers have a way of knowing what works and what doesn't and the quads soon became indispensable work buddies. The quad filled a niche where larger vehicles could not go. Soon, the British Ministry of Defence was ordering them on an urgent operational requirement, making official what the soldiers on the ground already knew.

The quads were used to carry out several roles, including the resupply of water or ammunition, or for CASEVAC duties with specially adapted trailers

HELMAND DEPLOYMENT
British soldiers from 3rd Battalion, Parachute Regiment deploy on their Yamaha Grizzly quad bikes in Helmand province, Afghanistan. The quad bike proved to be a reliable and useful operational tool for the elite soldiers, as well as for special forces.

SPECIAL FORCES QUAD BIKES
US Army special forces
soldiers ride quad all-terrain
vehicles across a desert plain
during an operation in 2002 in
the village of Daste Arche in
northern Afghanistan.

that could carry stretchers. The quads could get the wounded back to a field hospital or a helicopter much faster than four or six men carrying a stretcher and equipment.

Apart from essential resupply and CASEVAC duties, the quads could also be used proactively on missions such as ferrying snipers to high ground or other interventions that drew on their speed and mobility over rough terrain. It is not surprising that special forces soon took an interest in these light, low-profile machines.

The advantage that a quad has over a motorcycle is that it is essentially a more stable platform that provides greater security to the operator. On a motorcycle you need to be paying attention at all times to where you are going, whereas a quad allows the operator to look around as well as respond more quickly to any threat. The operator can deploy their personal weapon more quickly or use a weapon mounted on the vehicle.

While the British Army selected the Yamaha Grizzly and the United States military largely opted for the Polaris MV850, other innovative manufacturers, such as the Netherlands' Defenture and Britain's CCM Motorcycles, have also seen the opportunity for bespoke special forces variants. These are likely to take on an increasing role next to their two-wheeled cousins.

John Deere M-Gator A1

The M-Gator has been in service with the US Army, US Marine Corps, Canadian Defence Force and Belgian Army and has been deployed to Afghanistan and Iraq. It has a reinforced hull and can carry a payload up to 748kg (1649lb). Its inherent strength also allows it to be air-dropped and to cope with rugged terrain.

JOHN DEERE M-GATOR

Country of origin: United States

Manufacturer: John Deere

Service: 1997–present

Operators: US military

Crew: 2

Weight: 658kg (1450lb)

Dimensions: Length 2.74m (9ft), Width 1.52m (5ft), Height 1.09m (3ft 7in)

Powerplant: 3-cylinder diesel

Range: 250km (155 miles)

Speed: 30km/h (18.6mph)

Weapons: N/A

The engine and front rack are positioned forward of the driver and passenger, and there is a load area at the back. It has a bumper at the front with an integral brushguard. It also has a roll-over protection system.

It is powered by a Yanmar three-cylinder, liquid-cooled, four-cycle diesel engine, which is coupled to a continuously variable transmission (CVT). The engine can run on either diesel or JP8 fuel.

The M-Gator is fitted with rack and pinion steering and has a fully independent A-frame suspension. The low centre of gravity contributes to better handling at high speeds or on sloping terrain.

Other features include run-flat tyres and a winch. To bring it up to military specification, several alterations were made to the commercial off-the-shelf (COTS) version of the Gator. These include a military specification load bed, folding and lockable sides to the load bed, an M16-compatible rifle mount, black-out lights front and rear, military spec tie-down points and a mil spec bumper. The M-Gator is internally transportable in MH-47 and MH-53 helicopters, as well as the V-22 Osprey tiltrotor aircraft.

Polaris Sportsman MV850

The MV850 is the latest version of the Polaris ATV, following the MV700 and the MV800. The MV700 was in service with the US military between 2001 and 2007, after which it was replaced by the MV800.

POLARIS MV850
Country of origin: United States
Manufacturer: Polaris
Government and Defense
Service: 2013–present
Operators: US armed forces
Crew: 1
Weight: 444kg (978lb)
Dimensions: Length 2.42m
(94.5in), Width 1.2m (47.3in),
Height 1.52m (5ft)
Powerplant: 4-stroke SOHC
twin-cylinder
Range: 250km (155 miles)
Speed: 83km/h (52mph)
Weapons: Personal weapons
carried by operator

The MV850 is a four-wheel drive all-terrain vehicle designed to carry the operator and their equipment in challenging terrain and military conditions. It can carry up to 90.7kg (200lb) of equipment on the front rack and up to 181.4kg (400lb) on the back. It features a full underbelly skid plate and rugged front bumper.

Powered by a 77hp engine, the M850 can tow trailers laden up to 680kg (1500lb). The engine is also designed to provide braking power on descents.

The MV850 is fitted with electronic power steering and has a dual A-arm suspension with heavy duty shocks designed to carry the required loads over difficult terrain. Additional equipment includes an infrared (IR) light and a winch. Other accessories include cargo nets and a fender bag.

Scorpion 6.6 Tactical Diesel Quad

Manufactured by Defenture in the Netherlands, this quad has been commissioned for use by Dutch special operations forces (SOF). Powered by a multi-fuel diesel engine, the quad can be carried in the hold of an MH-47 Chinook helicopter for fast insertion. The quad features state-of-the-art

**SCORPION 6.6 TACTICAL
DIESEL QUAD**

Country of origin: The
Netherlands

Manufacturer: Defenture

Service: From 2023

Operators: Dutch Korps
Commandotroepen (KCT) and
Marine Corps (MARSOF)

Crew: 2

Weight: 1200kg (2645lb)

Dimensions: Length 2.53m (8ft
3in), Width 1.49m (4ft 9in), Height
1.27m (4ft 2in)

Powerplant: 2-cylinder diesel
common rail

Range: 600km (373 miles)

Speed: 75km/h (46mph)

Weapons: Personal weapons
carried by operator

suspension and an innovative four-wheel steering system which it is claimed sets a new benchmark for tactical air-transportable quads.

The deal with the Dutch Defence Materiel Organization (DMO) was against tough competition from market leaders such as Polaris, underlining the growing competition and interest in this sector of the defence market.

Yamaha Grizzly 450 IRS

The Yamaha Grizzly is a tough 4x4 quad bike that has been in service with the British Army for several years, including operations in Afghanistan. Having proven its worth in real fighting conditions, including service with the Parachute Regiment, the Yamaha Grizzly was confirmed as the official British Army quad.

Based on a successful commercial off-the-shelf (COTS) design, the Grizzly is a low-maintenance rugged quad with superb traction on different types of terrain. It has a fuel-efficient diesel engine linked to a three-mode on-demand transmission and has independent rear suspension. It is fitted with cargo racks and can tow a trailer that is adapted to carry stretchers.

YAMAHA GRIZZLY 450 IRS
Country of origin: Japan
Manufacturer: Yamaha
Service: 2008–present
Operators: British Army
Crew: 1
Weight: 281.2kg (620lb)
Dimensions: Length 1.99m (6ft 5in), Width 1.09m (3ft 6in)
Powerplant: Diesel 450cc
Range: N/A
Speed: 75km/h (46mph)
Weapons: Personal weapons carried by operator

GLOSSARY

A400M: Airbus turboprop military transport aircraft

AFSOC: Air Force Special Operations Command

AGL: Automatic Grenade Launcher

ATGM: Anti-Tank Guided Missile

ATV: All-Terrain Vehicle

CH-53 Sea Stallion: Sikorsky US Marine Corps heavy-lift helicopter

C130: Lockheed Hercules turboprop military transport aircraft

C4ISR: Command, Control, Communications, Computer, Intelligence, Surveillance and Reconnaissance

CASEVAC: Casualty evacuation

CROWS: Common Remotely Operated Weapon Station

CSAR: Combat Search and Rescue

CTIS: Central Tyre-Inflation System

CV-22: US special operations forces variant of US Marine Corps MV-22 Osprey tiltrotor aircraft

DMV: Desert Mobility Vehicle System

ECM: Electronic Countermeasures

E-WMIK: Enhanced Weapon Mount Installation Kit

FOB: Forward Operating Base

GPMG: General Purpose Machine Gun

GMG: Grenade Machine Gun

GMV: Ground Mobility Vehicle

GMV-M: GMV MARSOC

GMV-N: GMV Navy

GMV-R: GMV Rangers

GMV-S: GMV Special Forces

GMV-ST: GMV Special Tactics

HMG: Heavy Machine Gun

HMMWV: High Mobility Multipurpose Wheeled Vehicle 'Humvee'

HMT: High Mobility Transport

HSUV: Hardened Sports Utility Vehicle

IED: Improvised Explosive Device

IFAV: Interim Fast Attack Vehicle

IFOR: Implementation Force

IR: Infrared

ISAF: International Security Assistance Force

JLTV: Joint Light Tactical Vehicle

JOC: Joint Operations Command

JP8: Jet Propellant 8 aircraft fuel

JSOC: Joint Special Operations Command

JSOTF: Joint Special Operations Task Force

KSK: *Kommando Spezialkrafte* (German special forces)

LMTV: Light Medium Tactical Vehicle

LRDG: Long Range Desert Group

LRPV: Long Range Patrol Vehicle

LSV: Light Strike Vehicle

LTTV: Light Tactical Transport Vehicle

MAPK: Modular Armour Protection Kit

MARSOC: Marine Special Operations Command

M-ATV: MRAP All-Terrain Vehicle

MEDEVAC: Medical Evacuation

MPV: Mine Protected Vehicle

MRAP: Mine Resistant Ambush Protected

M-WMIK: Mobility Weapons Mount Installation Kit

NORSOF: Norwegian Special Operations Forces

NSCV: Non-Standard Commercial Vehicle

NSTV: Non-Standard Tactical Vehicle

NZ SAS: New Zealand Special Air Service Group

OAV: Offensive Action Vehicle

ODA: Operational Detachment Alpha

ODB: Operational Detachment Bravo

OEF: Operation Enduring Freedom, Afghanistan

OIF: Operation Iraqi Freedom

PB: Patrol Base

RIMA: *Régiment d'Infanterie de Marine* (French Marines)

PMV: Protected Mobility Vehicle

QRF: Quick Reaction Force

RCWS: Remote-Controlled Weapon System

RSOV: Ranger Special Operations Vehicle

RWS: Remote Weapons Station

SAS: Special Air Service

SASR: Special Air Service Regiment, Australia

SATCOM: Satellite Communications

SBS: Special Boat Service

SF: Special Forces

SFOD-D: Special Forces Operational Detachment-Delta

SFOR: Stabilization Force

SFTG: Special Forces Task Group, Australia

SOAR: Special Operations Aviation Regiment

SOF: Special Operations Forces

SOG: Special Operations Group

SOTG: Special Operations Task Group

SOTV: Special Operations Tactical Vehicle

SOV: Special Operations Vehicle

Spesialkorpset: Danish special operations forces

SR: Special Reconnaissance

SRV: Surveillance and Reconnaissance Vehicle

ST: Special Tactics

UANSCV: Unarmoured Non-Standard Commercial Vehicle

UKSF: UK Special Forces

USSOCOM: United States Special Operations Command

WMIK: Weapons Mount Installation Kit

Weapons

AT4: 84mm (3.3in) anti-tank weapon

BGM-71: Tube-Launched Optically Guided (TOW) anti-tank missile

GAU-19: three-barrel rotary machine-gun .50 BMG

GPMG: UK military L7A2 General Purpose Machine Gun 7.62mm (0.3in)

Javelin: AGM-14 anti-tank missile

M2: US military .50 calibre Browning machine gun

M240: US military version of FN MAG 7.62mm (0.3in) medium machine gun

M249: squad automatic weapon/light machine gun adapted from Belgian FN Herstal Minimi

M60: US military 7.62mm (0.3in) general purpose machine gun

MAG: *Mitrailleuse d'appui général*

MAG58: General support machine gun 7.62mm (0.3in)

MILAN: *Missile d'Infanterie léger antichar*: anti-tank guided missile

Mk 19: 40mm (1.6in) grenade launcher

Mk 47: Striker 40mm (1.6in) grenade launcher

INDEX

References to images are in *italics*.

PICTURE CREDITS